WHAT PEOPLE AF

MW01291916

"*I WAS VERY IMPRES*

subject could have been quite dry, but the experiences you added and the way you write made it very easy to read. I finished it in one sitting." – Cathy

"*EXTREMELY READABLE, this book is a treasure trove of useful tips for anyone moving country, or indeed just moving home. Writing from experience, Sara details every pitfall possible and how to avoid them. The inclusion of delightful photos personalizes the book. I would thoroughly recommend to anyone moving (or dreaming of moving) that they read this handbook. Absolutely excellent.*" – Alison

"*A MUST-READ for anyone contemplating a major relocation. It's packed with tips and tricks and lessons learned the hard way. Why not make your big move so much easier, for you, your loved ones, and even your pets?*" – Paul

"*As a millennial traveling abroad for a year, I'm joining a new community, city AND country every month. Sara's book has been hugely valuable to me, particularly the aspects that touch on how to cope with the stress of it all. I loved reading the personalized stories from fellow travelers. I would recommend this book as a MUST for any fellow traveler making a big move!*" – Maggie

"*This is the perfect book for everyone who'd like to start a new life abroad and is overwhelmed by all the tasks. Sara is giving you a hand in facing all those challenges and does her best in calming you down and structuring your relocation. I'm in love with the lists she created, resources, required reading, apps you can use…it's so helpful and makes it so much easier to navigate the bureaucracy jungle. I would love to have had this book before I started my digital nomad life.*" – Julia, wifitribe

"I am kind of a freak about organization so the prospect of cleaning, organizing, and boxing up my flat is pretty exciting for me, but your list of 'pain points' were things that I hadn't considered. I've read the chapter on pet relocation about ten times over as moving my cat is probably my greatest worry. Not only how to transport him, but also how to make him feel comfortable and secure in our new home that will also be completely new to me. I have also bookmarked Chapter 16's 'Final Countdown' to help prepare myself practically and mentally. I'm really thankful to have this information laid out so accessibly!" – Rachel

"Sara's voice shines through as she provides incredibly useful information that makes the thought of moving quite manageable. A smart layout ensures the content is extremely easy to absorb. It's the perfect guide for anyone on the move!" - Kaaren

"I love it! Honestly there is so much to take from it and, between your advice and the numerous life stories, it was so comforting; like I was being talked to and learning, rather than being talked at. I feel much more confident about the idea of relocation after reading this guide." - Lindsay

"I recently moved to a new city and I found this guide very helpful in keeping me organized and sane. Highly recommend to anyone making a big or small move!" – Kelsey

"A great guide and companion for anyone making a big move. It is an enjoyable read and highly accessible. Honestly, it's like Sara is sharing her wisdom in the comfort of your living room over a nice hot cup of green tea. Insightful as much as it is comforting. The stories are all great and the tips are invaluable. I would highly recommend How to Make Big Moves if you or people you care about are relocating." - Jodi

HOW TO MAKE BIG MOVES: RELOCATE WITHOUT LOSING YOUR MIND

A GUIDEBOOK FOR THE MINDFUL MOVER

SARA GRAHAM

ISBN: 978-1-7168-8309-5 (sc)
ISBN: 978-1-7168-8308-8 (e)

Because of the dynamic nature of the Internet, any web addresses or links contained in
this book may have changed since publication and may no longer be valid. The views
expressed in this work are solely those of the author and do not necessarily reflect the
views of the publisher, and the publisher hereby disclaims any responsibility for them.

Any people depicted in stock imagery provided by Getty Images are
models, and such images are being used for illustrative purposes only.
Certain stock imagery © Getty Images.

Lulu Publishing Services rev. date: 07/08/2020

To Mario – my love. Without you this project would have no inspiration. Thank you for giving me a reason to make big moves. This relocation story is definitely not over!

To my family in New Zealand, my friends in Canada and Bermuda, and all the wonderful people I have met in between. Especially those 40 individuals who backed the *How To Make Big Moves* project through Kickstarter! Thank you for your generosity and support.

To two exceptionally talented women – Charlene and Paulina – infinite gratitude for hanging in the crazy creative space with me.

While this guide is meant to be fun and lighthearted, I want to acknowledge those that are, in great numbers, forced to relocate because of war, disease, government unrest, and a myriad of other unfortunate circumstances. The thought of not feeling free and safe in one's homeland is a kind of desperation that should not exist. And then, as my brother Dan lamented on a Skype call, "borders are not so fluid" for those hoping to create a new life. Immigration is indeed a complex issue – one of the most contentious topics of our times - and I implore you, dear reader, to educate yourself on the current situation. Locally and globally.

While governments may be slow to enact laws that provide fair opportunities for their residents and citizens (to which two very different sets of laws apply), you can extend a peaceful hand. Whether offering language lessons, teaching yoga, or volunteering… the method does not so much matter as the intention to create a better world where people can thrive, rather than feel threatened. Deepak Chopra and Gabrielle Bernstein do a wonderful job of demonstrating that we are all connected in this universe. I have suggested a few of their online resources and books within this guide.

Who Is This Guidebook For?
The content of this guide is made up of focused intelligence for the soon-to-be expatriate. For all intents and purposes, an 'expat' is defined as someone living outside of their native country for at least six months of a 12-month period. We're talking about lifestyle migrants looking for a fresh start in a totally foreign environment. That said, if you fall into one of the following groups, you will probably benefit from the information and tips within.

So are you …

- a millennial on the move after graduation from college or uni?
- a corporate employee relocating for work?
- an entrepreneur/freelancer looking for a change of scenery?
- currently living as an expat?
- moving for your partner's career?
- moving to further education?
- moving for an internship?
- moving to another city within your native country?
- planning a sabbatical or working holiday?

I may have missed one or two categories here, but these are the people who will gain the most from using this resource.

Download & Organize

To supplement the chapters, there is a handy (and I must say beautifully designed) printable **workbook** that you can download at www. howtomakebigmoves.com. The 10 checklists and cheat sheets are guaranteed to get your head in the game and make the whole process a little less painful.

Away we go!

CONTENTS

Chapters 1-8 RELOCATION 101
Your Burning Questions Answered

1. Why & Where 1
2. Common Misconceptions & Culture Shock 7
3. Working Abroad 13
4. Citizenship & Residency (And Those Damn Taxes) 25
5. Cash Money (A Bit About Banking) 35
6. Healthcare & Insurance 41
7. Language 51
8. Home Hunting 56

Chapters 9-10 RELATIONSHIP MANAGEMENT
With Others and With Yourself

9. Family, Friends & Social Media 61
10. The Chakra Effect 66

Chapters 11-18 MAKING THE BIG MOVE
Let's do this!

11. Selling Your Stuff 80
12. Making The Big Move | Shipping 86
13. Pets 96
14. Packing/Unpacking 105
15. Tech Support & Security 111
16. The Final Countdown 116
17. Networking (Aka. Get Off The Computer!) 121
18. Final Words of Advice 125

THE WORKBOOK | Helpful (Printable!) Lists
AVAILABLE AT HOWTOMAKEBIGMOVES.COM

i.   Download and Disconnect List
ii.   Selling, Donating & Giving Away
iii. Master Packing List
iv.   Shipping Declaration Form
v.   Chakra Cheat Sheet
vi.   Checking In and Setting Up List
vii. Tracking Expenses
viii. First Shopping Lists – Food & General
ix.   First Shopping List - Room x Room
x.   Cheat Sheet for Recyclables

CONTRIBUTORS

Anne-Marie Bodal Design Director: UK to South Africa to Singapore to Thailand to Spain to Australia
Anne Samulevicius UK to France to Canada
Ashleigh Dempster Founder, AKID BRAND, Toronto to LA
Ling (Charlene) Lo Program Director at Hollyhock, Toronto to Hong Kong to Vancouver
Bryan Tomiak Sales Manager, GeoBlue, USA
Christie Berlin Accountant, Sweden
Franco Freda Composer & Sound Designer, Argentina to Sweden
Mickey Rapkin Writer & Author of *Pitch Perfect*, NYC to LA
Mirko Marino Sales Manager, AGS Movers, Prague
Paul Andersen CPA, Canada
Rachel B Velebny Freelance Writer USA to Czech Republic to UK to the Netherlands
Ross Belfer Co-Founder and CEO of Xhibition PR, USA to Israel
Ted Graham Owner, Queenstown Ice Arena, Bermuda to New Zealand

INTRODUCTION

OK, so I know your first question is: *Who are you?* And the next is: *What authority do you have to write about the hugely complex topics that revolve around relocation?*

Lean in and I'll try to get through this bit quickly.

Sara Graham here. I currently live in Vancouver with my husband Mario and three cats named Tigerlily, Dragon and Lion. I'm self-employed and run a brand development + communications business. More on all this at www.freshpresse.co. Before I made the leap to a laptop lifestyle, I was editor-in-chief of two teen magazines. And before that I was in fashion marketing and, for a three-year stretch, had my own underwear collection. Admittedly I have been a little all over the place career-wise, but underneath it all I am a planner... Organized to a fault and, where relocation is concerned, this is actually an asset. I am also diagnosed OCD so I apologize now if I have gone a little "extra" on some things, but I am hoping my all-angles attitude will take you places.

Throughout this guidebook, I'll give you key learnings (and work-arounds) from my own experience moving from Toronto, Canada to Prague, Czech Republic, and then (16 months later) Uppsala, Sweden. Mario has lived in Florence, Rome, Brussels, Amsterdam and Toronto (where we met) and his job as a 3D character artist is the reason we've been on tour.

Tips from my family will be also be included. *Why*, you ask?

Here is the short answer: My father grew up in Manitoba, moved to Bermuda when he was 16, then went back to Canada for university. After that it was back to Bermuda where he managed a reinsurance company, met my mother (a Canadian pharmacist on a work permit), and eventually took over his father's funeral business.

Another book, another time.

After raising three kids over 32 years, in 2009 they picked up and headed to New Zealand. Christchurch is their full-time home and, after eight years of bureaucracy, they're now NZ residents.

My brother Dan and his wife, Lenka, who is Slovakian, met in London and moved to New Zealand in 2009. They became citizens in 2019.

The youngest of us, Ted, first went to NZ in 2001 and had two stints at the university in Christchurch (2003 and 2007) before officially moving in 2009. He is also officially a citizen of that country, but still holds Canadian and British passports.

He and Dan own and operate an ice arena in Queenstown.

So imagine the piles of time and energy that has gone into moving this lot around… They have a few notes to share.

While I have traveled a whole lot, no trip could have prepared me for big moves to the Czech Republic, Sweden and Italy. It is a mind-bending, full body experience. You will, in fact, lose your mind at some point. My goal is to help you cope with your crazy. I have sourced information, ideas and advice from around the globe to help bring organization and a balanced mind into the mix.

The FIRST thing to note is that this process requires patience. A lot of it. Be prepared. Get on that meditation pillow if you must; it definitely helped me (see Chapter 10).

SECOND, a well-cushioned bank account is also essential. There are going to be expenses that no one could ever predict. Plus, the whole idea of moving someplace new is to actually enjoy a new environment, right?

The THIRD thing is to inform yourself in order to get really clear on what life (at least the aspects that are most important to you) will be like. This is not a romantic fling or some one-night stand where you can sneak off the next morning. No and no... you are *in this* and a deep commitment is required to relocate successfully.

Luckily you have this guidebook to help you through the big move!

Whether it's NYC to LA, London to Cape Town, or Toronto to Hong Kong, many of the contributors to this guide would agree that relocating to another city or country is a constant discovery mission. You'll think you have it all figured out, and then you need dental work. It takes several rounds, but you will eventually feel at home and at ease in your new environment. To that end, each chapter in this guide is structured to help you think ahead and, if you are super organized, create category-specific files on the prospective country: **Work, Finances, Healthcare, Social Networking** (offline networking too, of course) and so on. Same goes for all the stuff that needs to happen before you go anywhere: **Selling** and **Packing** and **Preparing** (this includes **Pets** if you've got a fur baby).

At www.howtomakebigmoves.com you will find a WORKBOOK that contains essential CHECKLISTS and CHEAT SHEETS. Download. Print. Use Them. File Them. These are part of your readily available documents (RAD).

IMPORTANT NOTES

- It would be damn near impossible for anyone to cover all expat scenarios in all countries. Where there is specific advice - either my personal experience or that of one of the contributors – it is meant to kick start your own thought process. So, where you might think the information does not apply, it does. You simply have to invest some time researching how it relates to where you are going.

- Further to that, use the RESOURCES section at the end of each chapter! Trust that I put hours into curating illuminating articles on relocation topics, the web pages with the most reliable information, as well as the best smartphone apps.
- If you get to the end and think I've glossed over a topic, or missed something entirely, then please let me know as I can potentially add it to the next edition. See the end of this guidebook for all my contact details.

Did I answer those two questions? Hope so because there is lots more ground to cover and we need to get back to the business of your big move.

Let's go!

CHAPTER 1

RELOCATION 101 | WHY & WHERE

"I moved to Cape Town in 2007 to experience life in a smaller city. I needed respite from living in huge pumping London. It's good for the soul and gives you space to focus." *Anne-Marie Bodal*

PEOPLE MOVE FOR all sorts of reasons; work, love, education, better opportunities, better weather, safety, lower cost of living, to learn a language, or just because they have been in one place long enough. Whatever the motivation, a lot of people are making the jump - including a record number of Americans considering leaving the US (Gallup Poll, 2019).

When I left Toronto for Prague in 2014 I was excited to escape the downtown grid I knew all too well.

I believe there has to be a strong internal drive to want to experience something different. It takes a lot of courage to up and leave that comfort zone. Over almost 20 years living in Toronto, working in fashion and media, I'd built a large social network -- the most difficult thing to replace in a new place.

From a macro-level perspective, the internet has allowed for a new kind of job freedom, and we've got a boom in 'lifestyle migrants' that is not slowing down. However, location independent living is not for everyone. Change is challenging in many ways.

But for those who are up for it, they'll say goodbye to slogging it out while getting snowed under, and discover a new happiness sitting pretty at a café in Costa Rica, or exploring Buenos Aires. Cool cities aside, new places offer a different perspective and can inspire new life chapters.

Naturally, there are sacrifices like being away from family, and benefits like being away from family. One has to strike a comfortable balance. Just remember you don't have to go away forever. Sometimes just one or two years can be enough.

WHERE
As far as the destination is concerned, lean in because there are places where the average person will do just fine (Czech Republic) and locations where only the moneyed will thrive (New Zealand). There are many questions one needs to ask, but I believe the TOP 3 are:

#1 Where will I have the best QUALITY OF LIFE?
#2 Where will my BUDGET go the furthest?
#3 Where can I raise CHILDREN?

Ok, so you might not be thinking about that third question so much, but it's a good sign when a country is highly rated in the *family well-being* category. For me, it indicates a happy society and a safe environment.

For future parents, the cost and availability of childcare, as well as education standards, are important things to consider.

Every year InterNations surveys thousands of people for their Expat Insider report. In 2019, 20,259 expatriates responded to provide insights on 187 countries. Here are some of the most fascinating findings... all countries listed in order of popularity.

Top Relocation Destinations: Taiwan, Vietnam, Portugal, Mexico, Spain, Singapore, Bahrain, Ecuador, Malaysia, Czechia.

Top for Quality of Life: Portugal, Spain, Taiwan, Singapore, Switzerland, Austria, Czechia, Finland, Israel, Japan, Canada.
★Countries ranked according to (1) leisure options, (2) personal happiness, (3) travel and transport, (4) health and well-being, (5) safety and security (6) digital life.

Top for Ease of Settling In: Mexico, Bahrain, Malaysia, Portugal, Philippines, Oman, Kenya, Spain, Ecuador, Costa Rica.
★Countries ranked on (1) feeling at home, (2) friendliness of the local population, (3) how easy it is to make friends and (4) how easy and important it is to learn the local language.

Top for Working Abroad: Vietnam, Czechia, Luxembourg, Germany, Netherlands, Norway, Estonia, Taiwan, Panama, Israel.
★Countries included and ranked in the areas of (1) career prospects and satisfaction, (2) work and leisure and (3) economy and job security.

Top for Personal Finance: Vietnam, Kazakhstan, Bulgaria, Mexico, Ecuador, Taiwan, Malaysia, Panama, India, Columbia.
★Countries ranked on expats rating their personal finances relative to disposable household income covering all living expenses.

Top for Cost of Living: Bulgaria, Vietnam, Ecuador, Mexico, Ukraine, Poland, Malaysia, Portugal, Spain, Columbia.
*Countries ranked on expats' satisfaction with the cost of living in their host country.

Top 5 for Family Life: Finland, Sweden, Belgium, Austria, Czechia.
*Countries ranked according to (1) availability of childcare and education, (2) costs of childcare and education, (3) quality of education, and (4) family well-being.

Safety & Security

Ah, to feel safe and at peace in a country where the politics and economy are stable… these are cornerstones of *la dolce vita* and ultimately feeling "at home".

In general, urban safety has taken a bit of a beating in recent years with riots, disease, natural disasters, and cybercrime all putting a strain on infrastructure. A complex issue, indeed; especially because every region of the world is going to see greater urbanization over the next 30 years. For the latest intel, I looked to the Safe Cities Index 2019. The Economist Intelligence Unit (EIC) report is "based on an index composed of more than 57 quantitative and qualitative indicators. These indicators are split across four thematic categories: digital security; health security; infrastructure security; and personal security."

Because only 60 cities have the data available, this is not a comprehensive list, but it can still give us a good look at where people are sleeping safe and sound.

The PS on Personal Security… There are tips on how to protect yourself from fraud and identity theft in Chapter 15.

Overall:

Tokyo is #1, then Singapore, then Osaka. These Asia-Pacific capitals are followed by Amsterdam, Sydney, Toronto, Washington DC, Seoul and Copenhagen tied for 8th, and Melbourne rounds out the top 10.

To download the full Expat Insider 2019 Report, go to www.internations. org/expat-insider/.

The Economist's Safe Cities Index is available at www.safecities. economist.com/safe-cities-index-2019.

Big data aside, you want to be 100% certain that your income will exceed the cost of living in your prospective country. Factoring in taxes, of course. I dig into this in Chapter 4, but allow me to get a couple things out of the way. First, be very aware of source of any stats and reports you read on expat living. For example, one 2014 survey by a reputable international bank "revealed" that New Zealand was #1 for raising children abroad. *Really?* Well, if you talked to the average person in NZ you'd discover that, while the country sure is safe, the cost of living is outrageously high and wages are not keeping pace. My point is that you certainly don't want to rely on this sort of data in the decision-making process. Make sure you back up and check exactly who was surveyed. Expats given sweet high-paying placements by multinational employers are going to have opinions far removed from the average individual.

Another, and let me say far more reliable, resource would be cost of living statistics. Mario and I use NUMBEO.COM to gather current data that paints a full picture of the major living expenses.

While you are at it, skim the EXPAT ARRIVAL GUIDE offered by your country of choice (often available online), and search reliable sources for LOCAL NEWS.

ROSS' MOVE

Being born and raised on the US East Coast, I've spent the majority of my life in the same place (a radius of about three-hours drive) - whether it be my childhood, college education, or first dive into "careerism" in NYC. Since my personality developed to specifically embody constant energy, moving about and exploration with no boundaries or limits therein, a special wave of anxiety and stagnancy during the brutal and sunless Northeastern winter was what first sparked my interest in moving abroad. As a coincidence, my career and profession of choice turned out to be travel PR and, from the moment I was 22 up until 28, I worked for the same company as a publicist and account exec for luxury hotels and destinations, specifically culturally-rich Israel. When I discovered that the Israel Ministry of Tourism had no representatives with my specific media training living in the country; no one to greet and work with journalists upon their arrival, I saw a golden opportunity to implement my skill set in a new role oversees. A blessing. I saw this self-realized opportunity and was set on relocating oversees for a one-year period. To ensure I would exit NYC for a period of time, I applied and was accepted to Tel Aviv University's MA in Conflict Resolution and Mediation. I used this acceptance as a final ultimatum to myself to follow my dream and move abroad for a taste of a different life, at least for a period of time. Four years later, a master's degree under my belt, and more than three years working with North and South American journalists arriving in Tel Aviv, I am currently the Co-Founder and CEO of Xhibition creative agency. In Oct 2014 we started with two people (myself and a partner), and two clients. Today, we are a staff of 12 and have 40 clients worldwide. *Ross Belfer*

FOLLOW @howtomakebigmoves on Instagram

CHAPTER 2

RELOCATION 101 | COMMON
MISCONCEPTIONS & CULTURE SHOCK

LISTEN, JUST BECAUSE you move hundreds or thousands of miles away, does not necessarily mean you're born again and all your past troubles are going to magically evaporate. More problems can potentially develop if you are not prepared mentally and emotionally for the challenges that invariably arise.

While the thought of a "fresh start" can be intoxicating, we, as humans, crave connection with others. Remember how long it took to find good friends in your homeland? The people you can really count on and trust. Years, right? It's going to take some time to integrate and find your people in the new society.

An excerpt from an article I wrote:

Patience. The necessity of a virtue, that I'm certainly not known for, was underscored in a Facebook chat with a friend who had relocated from Toronto to LA in 2011. If it took the beautiful, super social Ashleigh a year and a half to meet good mates, then I was in for a long haul given the language loops I was being thrown for.

Desperate for some kind of connection, I virtually reached out to friends in Canada. However, not being in the same time zone, I felt like I had disappeared from the collective consciousness. There were kids and divorces on top of full-time jobs, after all. And I had none of these things. To them, I hypothesized, I was "living the dream" and that's all they needed to know. Period. Fair trade.

It's true that I did not start to feel like I was making solid connections until around the 14th month mark. Chapters 9 and 17 of this guidebook have advice on how to get through. For now, I can offer these before-you-go tips...

GET SOCIAL! Take the time to reach out to as many people in your prospective country as possible, across a range of income brackets. Use Facebook (there is bound to be a friend of a friend) and LinkedIn to connect. Don't drive people crazy, but don't be afraid to ask your key questions. Who knows, you might just score a dinner invitation even before you leave.

READ UP! Check out news information sites like TheLocal.it/se/es/dk etc. There are eight editions that provide news in English for European and Nordic countries. Others like PraguePost.com are worthy sources. Searching within country- or city-specific expat groups on Facebook, you are bound to find links to topics that are currently trending.

CULTURE SHOCK

Arriving in a new place is complete sensory overload. Things that were so simple suddenly require more mental bandwidth. And, oh, all the unwritten rules! You are going to feel overwhelmed.

Before you go, make time to Google the norms of the society you will be walking into.

TIP | Skip out of date blog posts and join expat Facebook groups as they're a goldmine of current information and a great place to ask questions. Be wary of strong opinions, of course. There will always be someone eager to put a negative spin on a topic. Always triple check any advice given, especially when it comes to things like visas, work permits and tax rates. And lastly, don't bother with groups that have thousands of members, but zero engagement on posts.

With those warnings out of the way, know that there are *many* different types of groups out there:

- Want to know how others from your homeland moved to a specific country? Join a group like 'Canadians living in Mexico'.
- Want to know about life in a particular country, join a group like 'Life in France for Expats' or 'Moving to New Zealand' that have global membership.
- Groups like 'Foreigners living in [insert city]' or 'Expats World in [insert city]' will get you connected with people who can share city-specific information.

And then groups splinter out into special interests where you can meet local hobbyists or activists, and there are loads of women-only groups as well. Just choose your city or country and start searching!

By packing useful insight on what to expect in your back pocket, you will gain confidence and feel a few steps ahead in the process.

Worth saying again: Beware of questionable intel.

Obviously doing business is a whole other ballgame and you want to be up on what is acceptable culture. In Italian business circles, for example, the double-cheek kiss is seen as way too friendly. Go figure.

Here are other cultural curiosities that came up in a related thread that I started on the InterNations forum[*]:

- Long lunches followed by naps in Southern France. Everything stops between noon and 2pm.
- While it's a double hit in France and Italy, three kisses is a common greeting among the Swiss, as well as Serbians. Although in both countries' business circles, this practice has become unpopular in the last decade.
- Swedes always take their shoes off when entering a home. Mario actually takes his off at the office too. Make sure your socks are clean!
- Indians nod their heads in the same direction for 'yes' and 'no'. A little clockwise (or counter-clockwise) movement means 'ok' or 'it's done'.
- In the Middle East, bad news is often delayed as people don't like to criticize.
- Israel's workweek is Sunday to Thursday.
- On Mainland China, manners can be somewhat questionable and you can find more than one YouTube video highlighting

---

[*] These are opinions of individuals and do not represent InterNations as a community or company.

lovely things like parents letting their children relieve themselves in public.

On the flip side of these bad habits, lies a boom in Western etiquette training. While it's the nouveaux riche dropping thousands of yuan on "hostessing" courses, in October of 2014, the Chinese government issued a strict travel advisory to the average citizen traveling abroad. Behave or be blacklisted.

FRANCO'S MOVE

When I relocated to Sweden, I had already been living in three completely different places including Australia, the UK, and my home country Argentina. Each of these places have very unique vibes, and peoples' behaviour was one of the clearest indicators of how cultural differences modify the way we perceive and interact with the world. Being a Nordic country, I expected people to be cold, somehow distant to outsiders, but was surprised by the opposite. The Swedish people enjoy some rituals, which are very important to get to know each other, like "fika", a sort of coffee break that can happen almost any time of the day.

One of the hardest things to get used to was the weather, of course. Especially coming from a country where temperatures rarely ever go under 10-5°C, but it also makes you appreciate ~~much more~~ going out in the sun when it's nice, or staying home to watch a movie when it's cold and dark.

Long gone are the bustling car honks and people talking loudly - two very common scenes in a city like Buenos Aires where I was raised. Instead, the urban landscape is quieter and more polite, as if it were shaking hands with you for the first time.

A quote from the Portuguese writer Fernando Pessôa has inspired me: "There comes a time when it is necessary to leave behind the clothes that hold the shape of our body and forget the paths that take us always to the same places. It is time for the journey. And, if we do not dare start it, we will have stayed forever on the fringes of our own selves."
Franco Freda

CHAPTER 3

RELOCATION 101 | WORKING ABROAD

LET'S OPEN THIS chapter with a little story about the Italian who arrived at Chicago's O'Hare Airport with a CV (and without a return ticket) in his bag. This poor soul thought he could just show up for the "American Dream" and find a job. Instead, the authorities swiftly shipped him back across the Atlantic. I know this tale is true because my guy knows this guy. Don't be that guy.

It is absolutely imperative that you are able to work, legally, in the destination of choice. While you might be a "visa-exempt foreign national" for travel, it is an entirely different matter for living and working. The fact is that you are going to require some kind of visa to spend an extended period of time in a foreign country. If you are going through a corporate relocation, then the HR department should be taking care of these details and you are free to proceed to the next chapter. Stay with me if you are interested in generating additional income once you have moved.

Skilled Workers Get Sponsored

Look into the country-specific programs for employment-based immigration. Canada and Australia will fast track visas for those who qualify as 'skilled workers'. To find out if your profession is eligible in those countries, respectively called *Express Entry* and *SkillSelect*, check out the links in the RESOURCES section at the end of this chapter.

Applicants need to prove relevant professional skills, English language competency, as well as meet health and character criteria. In addition, they need to prove guaranteed earnings.

See also Critical Skills Work Visa for South Africa, which also allows one to get a visa without a job offer.

Sweden also has a 'labour shortage list' that is published twice every year. Equipped with in-demand skills, this is the only way a non-EU job seeker can apply for work while in that country. Otherwise, you have to go home and apply for a work permit. But before that, a formal written offer of employment from a Swedish company is required.

Digital Economy Expats

We've all likely heard the term 'digital nomad', which refers to those that are using technology to work remotely. However, there is another segment that actually does the 9-5 (ish) office thing. There's a new generation of "boomers" made up of enterprising young men and women working to advance the internet economy. While e-commerce start-ups are flush with venture capital and private investment, traditional businesses are rushing to innovate with digital tools. Asia and Latin America are leading the charge; Singapore has also been steady in its evolution. If your interests lie in working for the next Amazon or Alibaba, start a review of the career opportunities with the likes of Rocket Internet (based in Berlin).

Stockholm is also showing its muscle; ranking as the 'best smart city' according to the 2019 Smart City Expo World Congress.

Entrepreneurs Enter Here

Whether you are already running an independent business, or you're thinking about cutting the corporate cord, you will want to do some research on those areas of the world that offer opportunities for entrepreneurs. One example is Hong Kong. This energetic city has an agreeable atmosphere for those who are into manufacturing goods. Between its shopaholic population and the vast array of high-quality production houses, you could be turning a profit very quickly.

On the other hand, you might have to get used to a different pace.

When I interviewed Rachel Brathen for Huffington Post about running her Yoga Girl empire out of Aruba, she said that it had been really hard to get used to everything being on "island time".

Despite challenges, the Swedish guru has successfully managed to grow her brand globally. Her husband is Aruban so no doubt that helped a bit, but she's got the tenacity, and now over 2M Instagram followers.

Aside from using social media to make connections, how do you determine the opportunities within your industry? The deep dive on this requires looking at big data trends, banking time doing online searches, and getting some on-the-ground intel.

For starters, we can look at things like LinkedIn's 2020 Emerging Jobs Report. This reviewed every public member profile that held a full-time position within a given country during the past five years. Once the talent pool was identified, LinkedIn then calculate the share of hiring and Compound Annual Growth Rate of this proportion for each occupation between 2015 and 2019 to identify job roles with the largest growth.

The results provide a snapshot of the jobs that are emerging.

Singapore – #1 ARTIFICIAL INTELLIGENCE SPECIALIST, #2 ROBOTICS ENGINEER, #3 FULL STACK ENGINEER
Germany – #1 AI SPECIALIST, #2 SITE RELIABILITY ENGINEER,
#3 CUSTOMER SUCCESS SPECIALIST
France – #1 DATA PROTECTION OFFICER, #2 ARTIFICIAL INTELLIGENE ENGINEER, #3 REAL ESTATE AGENT
UK – #1 ARTIFICIAL INTELLIGENCE SPECIALIST, #2 DATA PROTECTION OFFICER, #3 ROBOTICS ENGINEER
Australia – #1 ARTIFICIAL INTELLIGENCE SPECIALIST, #2 CYBERSECURITY SPECIALIST, #3 MARKETING AUTOMATION SPECIALIST
Canada – #1 ARTIFICIAL INTELLIGENCE SPECIALIST, #2 SITE RELIABILTY ENGINEER, #3 DATA ENGINEER
Brazil – #1 SOCIAL MEDIA MANAGER, #2 CYBERSECURITY ENGINEER, #3 SALES REPRESENTATIVE

To review the entire report go to www.business.linkedin.com/talent-solutions/emerging-jobs-report.

See the RESOURCES & REQUIRED READING section of this chapter for more links.

TIP | Madrid Protocol, International Trademark System. The Madrid System is a one-stop solution for registering and managing marks worldwide. File one application, in one language, and pay one set of fees to protect your trademark in up to 95 member countries.

VISAS & WORK PERMITS

"Immigration is a carousel. You have to jump in and hold on. The people that did not are not here." *Rachel B Velebny*

When it comes to obtaining the proper permissions to work, much depends on your passport and your unique circumstances. Read the fine print, research government web sites and, if necessary, make an appointment at the consulate or embassy of the country you are would like to move to. You want to be crystal clear on the protocol as it relates to the type of visa ('single' or 'multiple-entry'?) required, validity period and expiration date.

If single, or you and your significant other, have decided to go freelance and make the jump, there are work permits and trade licenses out there that allow one to set up shop. Note: These are NOT substitutes for a visa, which will allow you to live in a country. These sorts of licenses often require proof of income sources, and that you already have a bank account with a healthy balance. In the country.

Then, depending on your occupation, anticipated annual income, and who your customers are, you may be obligated to register for fun things like VAT (value-added tax - EU) or GST/HST (Goods & Services Tax/Harmonized Sales Tax - Canada). In New Zealand, IRD numbers are mandatory for anyone earning an income in that country.

Specific dates and deadlines all come into play so give yourself ample time when applying, and don't ever expect the process to be speedy. Brace yourself for the paperwork and don't put yourself in the position where you are scrambling.

WORKING HOLIDAYS

A working holiday is a grand way to test the waters around the world without needing sponsorship. Visa still required - most are offered under reciprocal agreements between certain countries to encourage travel and cultural exchange.

Possible restrictions are:

- Age may be set at 18 and capped at either 30 or 35
- Type of employment
- Length of employment
- Applicant must have sufficient funds to live on
- Health insurance required (in some cases the destination country will cover this).

One can easily find more information and access applications by Googling 'working holiday schemes'.

THE WORK-AROUND

Note that the following was only possible because my partner worked for a Czech company, and had a local bank account in his name, so we could pay rent and utilities.

In my case, I am a self-employed individual, who works with businesses around the globe. During the time we were in Prague, I was keeping my business outside of Europe so I never had a good reason to go through the process of obtaining a work permit/trade license, which would have allowed me to accept contracts in the Czech Republic.

My clients would pay me either via bank transfer, or PayPal, to an account in Canada. So yes, while living in Prague I retained my Canadian residency status and continued to pay taxes to the Canadian government. As you will come to understand, if you don't already, where your permanent residency is, is where you will pay taxes. More on citizenship, residency, and taxation in Chapter 4.

Holding an EU/British Citizen passport allowed me to live in the Czech Republic temporarily and without any additional permit, as long as I checked in with the immigration police. If staying more than three consecutive months (which I never did due to travel), I was entitled to apply for either a temporary residence certificate or permanent residence permit.

Advice for all the non-EUers coming up in the pages to follow (see *Rachel's Move*).

THE IMMIGRATION OFFICE

Not my idea of a fun way to spend a few hours, but it's a mandatory part of the process. In some parts of the world a translator may be required to get anything done.

Some offices are better run than others, of course. And while government workers and immigration police can seem rather apathetic to your needs, they are just doing their jobs to the best of their ability. Try not to lose your sh*t when your I.D. card application has been in the system for two months and the Swedish case worker, who is managing your file, decides to go on vacation. Twice. Once after asking for a document at 3pm on a Thursday - something that took a bit of time to scan – and after sending it at 5:30pm, we received her 'out of office for 10 days' auto response. And oh, our deadline for submitting the requested information was before she would be back! Sorry, I just turned that into a gripe. My point is, you are going to have WTF moments and you must remain calm.

Just make sure every document is time-stamped, either by email or at the office, CC the appropriate individuals, and everything should be fine.

My other point is that the time of year you are submitting your applications can work for, or against, you. If it was not already obvious, we were filing for our Swedish personnummers (I.D. cards) in peak summer vacation season. Things may have gone a little quicker in September. Whatever the weather, show up bright and early for best results.

Additionally, because Sweden was dealing with an immigration influx due to unrest in the Middle East, we were told it would take double-time to process our personnummer apps. Timing is everything and sometimes you really can't know anything until you are on the ground. The reality is that policies change all the time and it's tough to keep track.

Official government web sites are the only way to stay on top.

TIP | Provide original documents wherever possible. PDFs and photocopies of emails may not fly for things like proof of marriage or divorce. If you and your partner are not married, some proof that you have been together/shared a home may be requested. Mario and I really had to scramble to dig up old emails (Toronto and Prague landlords). Thankfully this was enough, but we just scraped by.

SCAMS
There are con artists after con artists in this world. Online and off. Be very careful trusting anyone offering "immigration representation". There are legit legal pros out there that are authorized, by governments, to charge a fee to represent those seeking visas, etc. And then there are the swindlers, who don't have any special connections or talents other than taking money (they will likely ask for upfront payment in cash). These sorts are looking for people who are willing to throw money at the situation, hoping someone else will deal with the paperwork. They won't care if you end up being denied (and unable to reapply for a year). In the case of many countries, Canada included, one does not

need to hire a rep to apply for a visa or for citizenship. Only authorized officers at embassies, high commissions and consulates can issue a visa, or not. The overarching message here is to be involved and aware of exactly what is required. There'll be some DIY, baby!

STEP X STEP

1. Start with government web sites – both the country you are leaving and going to.

2. Seek additional advice from an accountant, or lawyer, or licensed advisor – someone with integrity who is worthy of your trust. Most government web sites have (or will direct you to) a list of qualified and registered immigration advisors. Meeting these people and making sure they can answer the important questions is crucial. Take advantage of a free consultation wherever possible.

3. As mentioned in the introduction (you did read that, yes?), a cost of living analysis is essential and **Numbeo.com** is your best friend. This web site will quickly reveal if you will be able to live your desired lifestyle on the wages you will be making once you move. Or figure out how many extra side jobs you will have to get to make it work. Trust me, moving from Prague (very low cost of living) to Uppsala (very high) would not have happened if Mario could not negotiate the higher wage. It was like moving to another planet, especially when it came to having a beer out in a pub. I could not get drunk enough to numb the sticker shock.

RACHEL'S MOVE

After I graduated from the University of Idaho, my plan was to teach English in Prague for a year and then go back to the States and get a 'real' job. After two years in the Czech Republic I started to feel like I was building a home. I had friends, a job, an apartment. What did I have back home? Plus, I met my husband Tom around that time.

It's the general feeling in Europe that keeps me here... there is a safety and comfort living in the cities. For example, I love taking public transport, versus having to drive. The downsides are that Czech attitudes can be tough, and the immigration laws do seem to change a lot. For example, they became much stricter with visa approvals shortly after I got my very first one and a lot of people who arrived only a month later did not get approved. And at one time I was in a kind of visa limbo, not having one, but also not *not* having one. Luckily, I found a friend, a Czech/Canadian who charmed the visa officers. Eventually, through my husband, I was able to obtain a partnership visa, but not before they dropped by our flat to make sure we were a couple. With this kind of visa, I was finally able to find a job other than teaching and really start my adult life.

While I had help from friends, one thing I will say is do not pay an agency. Most agencies make promises they cannot keep and make the process seem much easier. In reality they cannot guarantee your visa will be approved, you will need to gather all the documents yourself, and you'll likely need to apply in person. I've seen agencies take advantage of fresh expats and their naivety.

If you can find a friend who has been through the process and is willing to help, trust them. It was frustrating to take time answering questions from new expats, using my hard-won experience to try and make their lives easier, only to see them find an 'easier' answer online. Most of those people were not able to stay in Europe as long as they would have liked.

It is impossible to know everything, but I do know that immigrating to another country is a carousel of bureaucracy. You have to jump on and hold on. And of course, blind confidence and luck will play a huge part! *Rachel B Velebny*

RESOURCES

- WorkPermit.com (a bit cluttered, but good information provided)
- Expatica.com
- Expat Explorer Survey www.expatexplorer.hsbc.com
- EURES – The European Jobs Network www.ec.europa.eu/eures
- Teaching English Abroad www.transitionsabroad.com/listings /work/esl & www.cic.gc.ca/english/Immigrate/skilled
- Australia www.border.gov.au/Trav/Work/Work/Skills-assess ment-and-assessing-authorities/skilled-occupations-lists/ CSOL
- New Zealand www.immigration.govt.nz & www.newzealand now.govt.nz
- South Africa www.bestjobs.co.za
- Sweden www.migrationsverket.se
- Czech Republic www.expats.cz/business & Czech Republic Trade License (Zivno) www.alexio.cz
- Canada www.cic.gc.ca/english/residents/iec/index.asp International Experience Canada (IEC) has three categories - *Working Holiday, Young Professional, International Co-Op Internship* - and provides young Canadians the opportunity to travel and work abroad. *IEC is also available to foreign youth who want to travel and work in Canada.

JOB SEARCH

www.indeed.com/how-the-world-works
www.rocket-internet.com/careers
Australia www.jobsearch.gov.au
Canada www.jobbank.gc.ca
Sweden www.swedishwire.com
UK (with excellent info on global job markets) www.prospects.ac.uk

REQUIRED READING

- The World's 10 Most Livable Cities www.dw.com/en/the-worlds-10-most-livable-cities-in-2019/g-50267607
- Business Etiquette www.dailyinfographic.com/business-etiquette-around-the-world
- Top Cities for Starting A Business (Movinga Report) www.notablelife.com/want-to-start-a-business-heres-where-you-should-live/
- The Best Job Search Apps www.thebalancecareers.com/best-free-apps-job-searching-2061001

FREE APPS

Good.Co (Android & iOS)

Indeed Job Search (Android & iOS)

Glassdoor – (Android & iOS)

SHARE Is the advice in this chapter working for you? Please post a review on the platform where you purchased the e-book or print copy.

CHAPTER 4

RELOCATION 101 | CITIZENSHIP & RESIDENCY (AND THOSE DAMN TAXES)

IN ORDER TO shine a light on the whole citizenship vs residency thing, I'll start with the big picture. Essentially, it is possible to be a citizen of multiple countries, and thus hold multiple passports, but you can be a permanent resident of only one. Operative word here is *permanent*. Yes, yes, loopholes and exceptions blah, blah... Let's avoid getting bogged down. I am not saying you can't be a card-carrying temporary resident of a country other than where your habitual abode is located.

It's all in the fine print.

CITIZENSHIP
This is what your passport is for. It indicates where you are a "national". Some might be wondering: *Do I have the right to apply for another citizenship?*

Well, first off, to gain citizenship one must prove a specified number of years as a legal permanent resident. Keeping in mind that dual/multi-citizenships are permitted among Commonwealth countries. Most EU countries allow it, but the Czech Republic, Denmark and the Netherlands have varied restrictions. Germany permits only EU and Swiss nationals to retain two passports. Norway bans it outright. Russia and the US accept the concept of dual citizenship, but are not so hot on the idea. While the former imposes strict laws around disclosure, the latter, well, it gets real complicated and I'll explain in a minute.

RESIDENCY

There is temporary and permanent with different rights attached. So, again I ask, *how far will your passport take you?* This is a good time to get crystal clear on that. While visa waiver (sometimes called *visa-free*) programs may allow you to stay in certain foreign countries for up to 90 days, or six months in some cases, there will be extended visitor visas and work visas you need to apply for in advance of travel.

If you are intending to extend the extension, with an eye on residency and officially becoming an expat, then there are forms for that and you can apply to adjust the conditions on the current visa.

Residency and work permits are so entangled it hurts to think about it.

I hold an EU passport (British citizenship through Bermudian birthright), and a Canadian one as well (thanks to my Canadian-born parents), so these do make life a bit easier based on where I have lived thus far. But then every EU country is different.

In Prague, I was permitted to stay on a tourist visa for three consecutive months; not entitled to work without a permit and had to formally apply for residency status.

In Sweden, the right to residency was automatic and I could work (or study) as soon as I arrived. All that was required was to obtain my personnummer/social security number (no fees), register as 'self-employed' with the tax office (no fees; approx 130 euro to patent a company name if desired), and I was in the system.

Like anyone with an EU passport, once we got to the five-year mark, it would be at that point Mario and I could apply for long-term residency status, or try to become Swedish citizens.

And then the sh*t hits the fan again.

All said, Canada does make it easy for its citizens to renounce and reinstate residency status. At the point where I was in the Swedish social system, and therefore paying taxes, it made sense to file the forms required to remove myself from Canadian residency and exonerate myself from filing tax returns in that country. The timing does not matter so much as both systems will weigh the days spent as a resident to determine the taxes due in each country. This is how double taxation treaties work. More on this soon.

Now there are some countries, like the USA, where residency does not come into play. Those living abroad, who retain their US citizenship and passport, still need to file taxes.

As I understand it, one pays out only on (worldwide) income in excess of $100k. So you might want to re-think the joint bank account thing... just saying. Note that one can renounce citizenship (and tax obligations) for a fee that, by the way, increased substantially in 2014. According to an article on Forbes.com, the 422% price hike (or 20 times the average in other high-income countries) was the State Department's response to the substantial uptick in expatriations.

In case you are curious, the only way an American can renounce US citizenship is by applying for a foreign citizenship with the intention to give up U.S. citizenship.

It's probably the right place to mention how important it is to keep your passport(s) updated and, at the very least, a year from expiry to be safe.

Many countries require it to be valid for six months beyond your intended return date.

So, say you are American and you're planning to live in Italy for six months. You've got to use your US passport to exit and re-enter the US.

Unfortunately, if you try to return on an expired passport you may very well be denied entry.

Canada won't even let you board the plane without a valid Canadian passport.

Likewise, dual US/Russia citizens are not permitted to leave Russia without a valid Russian passport.

Fortunately, if you realize this in time you can go to the appropriate Embassy, Consulate or government office to renew your passport.

Don't get stuck!

Should you remain a resident of wherever you are coming from?
Unless you are totally off the grid in Guatemala, or living off nuts and filtered water on a beach in Brazil, you best be paying taxes somewhere.

Residency is primarily an accounting issue. I.e. Where will you pay taxes? There are countries that have, let's say, more favourable tax rates, but it all depends on who you are and what you do for a living. One has to do the research to assess the full scope. Look closely at what you are getting for those tax dollars and what you will pay out for the things that are not covered, like healthcare and education for the children that you might very well have abroad.

Consult government web sites and your accountant if you've got one. He/she should be aware of the rules, as well as the treaties between countries that apply. For example, Canada and the Czech Republic have a treaty on double taxation that states if you are paying income tax in one country, you don't pay out in the other.

But then...

"It is possible to be a resident of more than one country for tax purposes. In that event, you can generally elect into residency in one country only under the provisions of the tax treaties between the countries.

Then you may have to pay tax in the other country(ies) on your source income from the other country(ies). Of course, there are exceptions and exemptions under the various treaties. You would be allowed to

claim a tax credit in your resident country for any tax paid to another jurisdiction. Clear as mud, but as simple as I can make it for you!"
Paul Andersen, CPA, Canada

TIP | If one has been taxed twice (on income that is eligible), they can claim Foreign Tax Credits, or what is known as Foreign Tax Credit Relief in the UK.

"Sweden has a complicated tax system with lots of ifs and buts. As a generalization, it has a progressive income tax rate ranging from 0% for salaries under 20,007kr/year up to 55% for salaries up to 1,644,100kr/year, and oddly 52% for salaries over 1,6 mkr.

The tax is a combination of state, county and municipality tax and an earned income tax credit is calculated at the end of each year. VAT varies between 6% for books, theatres and art, 18% for food and 25% for the rest. Health care is VAT free.

If you hire a company to perform repairs, conversions, extensions, cleaning, maintenance or laundry work you get a tax reduction up to 50% of the labour cost.

Although the taxes are relatively high, I keep reminding myself and my clients that we get almost free healthcare, 18.5% of our taxes go towards our pensions, we get 80% of our salaries (up to a certain amount) if we fall ill, are rendered unemployed, are on parental leave for 480 days and much more."
Christie Berlin, Accountant, Sweden

Sweden has a progressive income tax that is quite high. So high that the official Expat Arrival Guide uses the word *astronomical*. But compare this with the top marginal tax rate (33%) in California and one starts to understand that, actually, equal access to subsidized (and very good) health care and higher education, is worth something.

Expats living in France might express the same sentiments as Christie. There, once you are a resident for more than 183 days (roughly 6 months, not necessarily consecutive), taxes on worldwide income are due. The upshot is that residents have access to a very generous social system.

There are various salary calculators on the internet so you can figure out which countries are favourable to your income bracket.

Other notes on taxation:
- If you are an entrepreneur with a global client list, then there are tax implications for those clients when you change up your residency. To be sure you are invoicing according to the correct regulations, have a consultation with a local accountant.
- If you own property in the country you are moving away from, be sure it is worth keeping. The rental income may be attractive, but if you forget to pay the taxes on that income – on time – then the government will hit you with some pretty hard penalties. Likewise, if you sell a property *after* your residency ends. Case in point: My parents had been trying to sell a property located in Halifax for years. The sale finally went through when they had switched their permanent residency status to New Zealand. BFD. The taxes withheld by the Canadian government were significant. Timing is everything.
- Pay even closer attention when you are being taxed on your worldwide income. Double taxation treaties cover income tax on particular sets of earnings. Not necessarily capital gains on investments. Not necessarily property tax. Have a good look at the country's tax authority web site.

- Random intel: Australian employers are required to contribute 9.5% of an employee's base salary before tax to a superannuation fund. While this money is locked up tight for Aussie residents, temporary residents can apply to reclaim their superannuation funds when their expat stay has ended.
- Ask an expert! Remember what I said at the beginning? All situations in all countries would be impossible in this space. Get some trusted assistance on interpreting all the rules regarding your unique residency, citizenship and taxation guidelines.

CHARLENE'S MOVE

I never gave any thought about the subtle-but-major differences between residency and citizenship, or genetics and culture, until I uprooted myself from the only place I've ever known as home and became an expat in the only place my immigrant parents had ever known as home.

My birthplace is Canada, and my experience of this vast country was mostly contained within a couple hours of the Highway 401 in Ontario - namely London, Hamilton and Toronto. Of course I have traveled to both coasts and countless places in between, but in terms of living, studying and working, most of my 36 years were spent in one of these three cities.

Upon relocation to Hong Kong, China - the birthplace of my parents – all my senses were put in overdrive by new sights, sounds and smells around every corner. But within a few short weeks of living there, what struck me most were the new feelings when I roamed the streets looking in the eyes of passers-by and speaking to locals. I had spent my entire life looking different from everyone else, but feeling the same. Experiencing daily life the same way, speaking the same language and using the same lens to interpret the world. Now I suddenly looked the same as everyone else, but inside I felt vastly different. I shared neither the same views of the world, nor the same values. And, until recently, not even the same language.

So did this make me more Chinese or more Canadian? Which ethnicity did I identify with more? What was my culture? And furthermore, what was I to make of the difference between *residency* and *citizenship*? Having lived where I was born for most of my life, I used these words interchangeably. But when I landed in China and needed to get a visa and a Hong Kong Resident Card, it struck me that these terms are absolutely not the same.

Nature vs. Nuture vs. Nationality.
Of course, we are the sum of our experiences. Our points of reference and how we relate to new environments are directly informed by all our earthly interactions. I was born to Chinese parents. I grew up Canadian. Like a boomerang, I ended up in Hong Kong as a fully formed adult. And I lived there as a Canadian-born, Canadian-thinking, Canadian-speaking Chinese person.

I can proudly say that I went so that I could know my family of origin; my DNA, the Cantonese language, the intricacies of Chinese culture. My roots. Identity is our ego's way of finding our place in this world, and relocation can be the catalyst to deeply understanding all the complexities of who we are.
Ling (Charlene) Lo

RESOURCES *See Also Chapter 3 Resources*
- Returning to Canada https://travel.gc.ca/returning
- US Passport Guide https://www.us-passport-service-guide. com/can-i-reenter-the-us-with-an-expired-passport.html
- Double Taxation Treaties (EU countries only) www.ec.europa. eu/taxation_customs/taxation/individuals/treaties_en.htm
- Canada www.canada.ca (search 'tax planning' by province) & www.settlement.org (specific to Ontario, Canada but country government information well presented. Useful discussion forums too)
- Guide to taxes in France (and many other countries) – www.expatica. com/fr/finance/tax/A-guide-to-taxes-in-France_101156.html
- Expat bloggers from 139 countries www.expatsblog.com

REQUIRED READING
- www.nomadcapitalist.com
- www.forbes.com/sites/robertwood/2015/03/11/give-up-citizenship-keep-your-passport/

APPS
Deloitte tax@hand Customizable tax news and information resource for a growing list of supported countries and languages. Free on Google Android and Apple iOS.

CHAPTER 5

RELOCATION 101 | CASH MONEY
(A BIT ABOUT BANKING)

YOU NEED ONE of these. A bank, that is. Do some research and see if your current financial institution has any affiliates in what is to be your new hometown. You want a bank that speaks your language, has good hours, and even better customer support service both online and off.

Let's stick to two basic sets of information...

A. For the Big Mover staying in the same country
If you are running all of your financials through the interweb, and don't require a brick-and-mortar branch wherever you are going, then there is no need to switch up your bank. However, if your bank does not have ATMs where you are going then watch out for those annoying withdrawal fees from random cash machines. We've all been hit with extra charges from other banks' and unbranded ATMs. For this reason,

you may want to open an account with a local bank. Otherwise, keep your money where it is.

An option, for US citizens/permanent residents at least, is to set up an account with an online bank like Capital One 360. Transfer money out before closing your home accounts, et voila, you've got a national checking account set up for wherever you are going. No-fee cash machines included.

B. For the Big Mover switching continents

Setting up an account in another country can be quite a process. For example, when it came to setting up an account in Prague, it was as easy as walking into a bank with passport in hand. Whereas countries like the Czech Republic and Canada are a bit more flexible, in Sweden I had to wait to get my personnummer before it was possible to set up a bank account. By law, Swedish banks are supposed to let any passport-carrying individual open an account. However, the reality is most are picky and will hand you a hard time without the official ID card. It is a similar situation in Hong Kong with their identification cards.

You do not exist until you have one.

A contract with a reputable employer may satisfy the bank, as Mario discovered, until you receive such ID cards. It can also take what seems like an excruciating amount of time to get a credit card set up.

For these sorts of reasons, you may want to retain a bank account in your home country, as well as a credit card. If you are doing so, then make sure it is updated with your new address abroad. Some banks let their customers do this online, but some prefer you confirm any address changes in person. Same goes for credit cards. Check it.

CASH ECONOMIES

According to the Reserve Bank of India, 90% of all monetary transactions in India are in cash. Even Amazon localized its approach in India to offer COD as a service. India and other middle-income countries such as Indonesia and Colombia all have high cash dependence. But even where cash is still king, digital marketplaces are innovating at a remarkable pace. Nimble e-commerce players are simply working with and around the persistence of cash.

– *Where the Digital Economy Is Moving the Fastest*
by Bhaskar Chakravorti, Christopher Tunnard and Ravi Shankar Chaturvedi
February 19, 2015, Harvard Business Review

Germany is one of those places where "cash is still king". A 2017 study by the country's central bank, Deutsche Bundesbank, said Germans carried an average of 107 euros (over $115 at the 2017 exchange rate) in their wallet. That's more than three times what the average French person carries (32 euros), according to the European Central Bank. It is also far more than what Americans carry. Three-quarters of respondents in a U.S. Bank survey said they carried less than $50 — and one-quarter said they keep $10 or less in their wallet.

For the Germans, keeping cash on hand allows for better tracking of personal spending. They also put a high value on privacy and cash offers anonymity. According to NPR, "Cash Only" signs hang on front doors of many shops and restaurants in Berlin.

This is the case for even large transactions.

I do know a guy who, upon arriving from Canada, headed to Berlin's IKEA and proceeded to amass an entire apartment-load of furniture. He was not permitted to use his credit card at checkout. Burn.

Using PayPal? It's one account per country on this platform. You will have to open a fresh account that is attached to your new country's bank. If you are still banking through your home country, then no need to do a thing.

STEP X STEP

1. Find a new bank and set up an account before closing anything. In my case, my guy left months before I did and, since we had a joint account, I was able to transfer all funds to his new bank in the Czech Republic and close his chequing account in Canada. Easy peasy.

2. Your bank will ask which currency you want to transfer funds in. Recommend flipping to the currency of the country it is going to. In doing so you should avoid any funky "conversion" fees on the other end.

3. If you have a lot of money to move, pay attention to your bank's daily withdrawal/transfer limits. You may have to schedule final withdrawals, as you may not be able to take it all at once. There are laws in place to prevent a little thing called 'money laundering', which requires that banks and accountants report suspicious financial transactions and/or cross-border movements of currency. Not saying you or I would ever be involved in such crimes, but this is the world we live in and officials are increasingly on the lookout. Avoid raising eyebrows.

4. Unexpected fees always pop up so be prepared. Anything from closing money market accounts, to that auto payment (see #7) you forgot about, can cost you so try to mitigate additional stress by thinking ahead. I had one situation where a client could only pay by cheque (that I had to physically pick up) or wire transfer. Since I flying from Uppsala to Toronto was not possible, the wire transfer fees ended up being a significant amount - that I could have built into my initial job quote.

5. Make sure to have foreign currency in your wallet before leaving, and extra cash (USD, euros) on hand to convert if

needed. If you still have debit and credit cards attached to your home country bank, then be sure to call before departure to let them know you will be traveling.

6. Officially pay off and close any credit card accounts that you will no longer be using. Just because you cut it up the expired card, and did not activate the new one that arrived in the mail, **does not** mean the account is closed. Shutting it down can be done over the phone.

7. Deactivate any auto-renewals you have set up to your debit and/or credit card: Gym or social club memberships, as well as any online registrations. Even if your card is expired sometimes these charges go through and you will get an unwelcome surprise in the mail. *WTAF*, you say? Some companies, especially if the subscription has to do with a security feature, can override the system and charge without you getting any notice that "your card has expired, please change your account information".

This happened to Mario. Despite having closed all of his accounts in Canada, he had one anti-virus software registration on credit card auto-renewal. Wasn't using the product. Totally forgot about it. Burn.

TIP | Always do your online banking when you have a secure connection at your new home, not on open wifi at a café. Because that's just asking for trouble. Alternatively, using your smartphone's data connection is a better way to go when out and about.

RESOURCES

Closing Accounts www.wikihow.com/close-a-bank-account
Currency exchange www.XE.com

RELATED READING

- www.npr.org/2019/06/09/728323278/for-many-germans-cash-is-still-king
- www.theguardian.com/money/2015/aug/26/hsbc-closed-bank-accounts

APPS

XE Currency Convert 180+ currencies. Free on iPhone and Android
Mint A real-time look at all your account balances, plus ability to set up budget and bill alerts. Free on iPhone and Android
Expensify For those who are tracking work-related expenses in order to be reimbursed. Free on iPhone and Android
TransferWise A great service for international money transfers.

CHAPTER 6

RELOCATION 101 | HEALTHCARE & INSURANCE

"Look into local coverage first. A lot of people don't know about ACC [Accident Compensation Corporation] in New Zealand, which provides no-fault personal accident insurance. This essentially covers anybody for any accident. Good to know for those living in the country, and also when you have family visiting." *Ted Graham*

PRIVATE, GOVERNMENT- OR STATE-SUBSIDIZED... Your options will depend on your nationality or residency, or what your employer has set up for you, or a combination, or there may be nothing limiting what healthcare services you do or don't have access to. The latter absolutely applies to emergency medical care, which any hospital anywhere is obligated to provide. Sometimes free, sometimes for a fee.

My extended family has tested the medical systems in Bermuda, Canada, the UK, the Czech Republic, Sweden, Italy, New Zealand, Australia, Iceland and Slovakia. What all this experience boils down to is that there is very good healthcare available. Many governments provide the basic care that most people require – at zero or very low cost once work permits and/or residency status is acquired. One only needs to be informed on the rules of the respective country.

EXAMPLES

In Canada, healthcare coverage varies between the 10 provinces and all permanent residents can apply for public health insurance. A health card is issued (typically within three months) by the provincial or territorial government and allows access to insured health care services.

Sweden offers those with personal identity numbers (personnummers) access to the exact same health services as residents and citizens. There's also this lovely price ceiling thing. This means that, after a patient has paid a total of between SEK 900 and 1,100 (depending on area of residence) in the course of a year, medical consultations are free of charge. There is a similar ceiling for prescription medication, so nobody pays more than SEK 2,200 in a given 12-month period. I paid SEK 115 (approximately USD$13) for each GP visit and not more than SEK 1,100 (approx US$127) in a year.

In New Zealand, once you are registered as living in the country with a two-year work visa, you pay as the locals do. Approximately NZ$50 per GP visit. Prescriptions are also subsidized and therefore relatively inexpensive.

Australia has an extensive state-subsidized system, called Medicare, as well as a private healthcare system that runs alongside it. Medicare has a reciprocal arrangement with the National Health Service in the UK and other European healthcare providers so citizens from those countries are instantly able to access some services.

In Italy, fees for things like dental care can be rather arbitrary across the country. One will often pay much more in the cities than in smaller towns for the exact same service.

PAY AS YOU GO

In my experience, with a bit of digging, I was able to find very good pay-as-you-go health services in Prague at manageable prices. Even emergency dentistry at the private Canadian Medical Care clinic (ironically) cost me less than it would have in Canada. When I needed a check-up on the lady parts, friends told me about a great doctor who charged a quarter of CMC's rates. While her office was definitely less modern, she got the job done efficiently and connected me with an (also very reasonably priced) ultra-sound clinic. This all required a bit more running around, but I saved a pile of Czech koruna.

When it came to dental work in Uppsala, as a new patient I was told I'd have to get in the queue (ugh) and wait between one and two years to get an appointment (what?!). Or try going to a less busy public clinic in the next town. Or go private. Either way, I'd be paying a higher proportion of costs (relative to general healthcare) before the state subsidy kicks in. Up to SEK 3,000 in this case.

DOES IT MAKE SENSE TO STAY ON A PAY-AS-YOU-GO SYSTEM OR BUY INTO AN INSURANCE PLAN?

Further to dental care in Sweden, EU/EEA citizens staying less than one year are entitled to use the emergency dental care services on the same basis as Swedish citizens, provided they are covered by health insurance in their home country and can produce a European Health Insurance Card.

So, yes, there are situations where investing in an insurance policy makes sense.

Case in point: Before Mario first arrived in Canada from Italy, he was told by his new employer to purchase health insurance from Blue Cross so he would be covered over the three-month gap before the Canadian government's coverage would kick in. He did not take that advice and, in the first month, he contracted a fairly serious eye infection. CDN$1,400 later …well, that point was made quickly.

In the case your new employer and/or the local government are not providing the health coverage that meets your needs, then you will have to look into extended plans. Same goes for self-employed types. It is necessary to have health insurance to obtain a trade license in Prague, for example.

In the end it all depends on your individual situation. As was apparent from Mario's case, insurance could have served him well in the interim. Furthermore, insurance can be a worthwhile investment to fast track access to services versus the agony of being put in a queue. Sometimes you really don't want to wait 90 days to see a specialist.

While us under-60-year-olds do have age at our advantage when it comes to investing in comprehensive coverage, note that plans can be rather pricey and there may be restrictions regarding which doctors you can visit. Double check the "Preferred Providers" list that usually comes with health insurance. Note that if you go to a doctor or hospital, which is not on the list, then your out-of-pocket expenses will be greater.

For example, Blue Cross has *Basic* and *Standard* options. The latter allows you to receive covered care outside the preferred network. Note that in an emergency situation, an insurer should not charge more for going outside of the network.

Credit Cards
Your credit card company may also offer coverage options so check in with their customer service reps before you take off. In my case, with my Canadian Visa credit card, I would be covered for any kind of medical emergency within the first 21 days of travel. The only caveat being that departure must be from Canada (ie. I'm not covered when flying out from Sweden).

Critical Illness & Life Insurance
Many banks offer life insurance policies, which may be something to consider as they cover a wide range of scenarios – from credit card debt to critical accident recovery. If you feel like you need this kind of backup then research the plans that might help your partner, or family, out if something happens to you. Again, the younger you are, the less you will pay. I kept the policy I set up in Canada as it does provide some international coverage, as well as hospital stays that might have happened while visiting Canada – handy during the period where I was no longer a resident and had given up entitlement to health insurance.

A Note on Supplements
When it comes to all-natural health supplements, you may find that your favourites are not available in your new country. For example, Melatonin is easy to find in Canada and Prague, but health shops in Sweden have been banned from selling it without a prescription... A bit mind-boggling if you ask me. Find out what you can and cannot get and stock up before you go!

Q & A WITH BRYAN TOMIAK AT GEOBLUE
Bryan has been working for international healthcare provider, GeoBlue, for over ten years and is the Direct Sales Manager for Individual Products.

Q. Does GeoBlue work with individuals as well as corporations to provide health coverage?

A. *Yes. GeoBlue provides travel medical insurance for individuals and their families, corporate groups, and also universities that have students, teachers, and faculty studying abroad a semester or longer. We also insure a lot of international students who are coming from other countries (especially China) to the United States to study for a semester or longer.*

Q. Focusing on Millennials and younger Gen X (aged 22 – 40), what kind of policies would you recommend for someone relocating to another country after graduation or for work?

A. *If they anticipate that they'll be living outside the US for more than six months, then I would recommend the Xplorer Essential or Xplorer Premier. The two plans are very similar with one major difference: Xplorer Premier offers worldwide coverage including comprehensive coverage inside the US, while the Xplorer Essential offers either basic US coverage (up to 3 trips back to the US up to 21 days each trip) or no US coverage (only international). The Xplorer Essential is roughly half the cost of Premier, mainly due to the fact that the cost of healthcare in the United States is typically much more expensive than many other countries around the world.*

If they happen to be living overseas as a student, teacher, or school faculty member (and not associated with one of the universities that we already have a student group plan with), then I would recommend our Navigator for Student plan. If they are living overseas to perform missionary work or working for a nonprofit NGO, then I would recommend our Navigator for Missionary plan. Both provide worldwide coverage, including within the US.

When our insured members are inside the US, our plans use the Blue Cross Blue Shield PPO network, which has a 95% doctors and hospitals participation rate.

Q. Most common policy/policies that expats purchase?

A. *For shorter term travel outside the US between 2 to 182 days, the Voyager Single trip plan is our top seller. The Voyager plan provides up to a $1,000,000* *medical limit and covers just about any sort of illness or injury that occurs while outside the US. It includes a medical evacuation benefit of up to $250,000. For clients living outside the US for 6 months or more, the Xplorer plans are the most popular.*

Q. Given that local insurers provide a certain amount of coverage, what are the advantages of tapping into GeoBlue and its global network? Eg. NZ's Accident Compensation Corporation (ACC) covers travelers and residents alike. Universal Medicare covers everyone in the UK.

A. *The majority of our plans have very comprehensive medical benefits and include coverage for pre-existing conditions and preventative care. Our Xplorer and Navigator plans have an **unlimited** medical benefit which most of our competitors don't offer. We take pride in making our plan benefits very straightforward and easy to understand. Many of our competitors have confusing or vague open-ended descriptions of benefits that can be misinterpreted easily. If the insured individual decides to challenge the ruling on a benefit decision, made by one of our offshore competitors, they are usually powerless since the company is not subject to strict US insurance industry standards. Our Global Health and Safety department provides 24/7/365 assistance to all of our 600,000+ members overseas with an array of services. All of our customers have a 24/7 collect phone number they can call for assistance with medical issues outside the US. We have doctors and nurses available around the clock. Furthermore, GeoBlue has an elite network of doctors from most every specialty in over 190 countries. We seek out professionals certified by the American or Royal Board of Medical Specialties who speak English, and we factor in recommendations by over 160 Regional Physician Advisors from all over the world.*

Another advantage: GeoBlue doctors and hospitals often bill us directly so our clients don't have to worry about filing a claim. Our members do not have to go to GeoBlue contracted medical providers outside the US and can select any doctor or hospital they choose and their benefits are the same. The main benefit of GeoBlue contracted doctors and hospitals outside the US is we can guarantee they are English speaking, Western training, and more likely to agree to direct billing. Our members also have the option to simply pay up front for the medical service and email us the bill, with a claim form, for reimbursement. State of the art online and mobile technology provides our members access to all their policy info including their medical ID card, automatically generated visa letters, up to date claim info, benefits, and more.

Q. Assuming you sell fewer insurance plans in countries offer "socialized" medicine (eg. Canada, Sweden), where is the demand for GeoBlue's services the greatest?

A. *Typically local plans only provide medical coverage within their immediate location and only within that particular country. They also tend to have fairly low medical maximums and rarely cover services at 100%. US expatriates living within countries that offer socialized healthcare, such as the UK and France, often still purchase medical insurance with GeoBlue for a number of reasons. Within socialized healthcare countries, the **free** medical treatment is only available at **public** medical facilities, not **private** facilities, which tend to be much higher quality and operate much more efficiency. I've heard many stories of patients going to public facilities with a medical emergency and having to wait more than six hours before receiving (often subpar) treatment.*

Q. What is the standard deductible? Does the potential policyholder have flexibility of choice?

A. *Our long-term "expatriate" policies such as the Xplorer and Navigator have calendar year deductible options ranging from USD$0, $500, $1,000, $2,000, up to $5,000. Another benefit of those policies is the deductible is waived for preventative care, like routine physical exams and vaccines, as well as for general practitioner and specialist office visits and filling prescriptions. You would generally only need to pay the deductible for more major services such as inpatient treatment, surgery, MRI, etc.*

Q. Can you share an actual scenario where GeoBlue came to the rescue?

A. *I have assisted with hundreds of cases where one of our members was severely injured in a location where the quality of the local healthcare was not adequate to* *effectively treat that particular medical condition. In such instances, we evacuate them using one of our air ambulance partners such as REVA or Flying Nurses. Our Xplorer and Navigator plans also include evacuation coverage for political unrest, states of emergency, and natural disasters. For example, we evacuated several members out of Fukushima, Japan after the tsunami damaged the nuclear reactors. We also evacuated a number of members out of Cairo, Egypt since their location was determined to be unsafe due to political unrest.*

TIP | Make sure the ICE 'In Case of Emergency' contact number is updated in your phone.

RESOURCES
BUPA www.bupaglobal.com
Blue Cross (USA) www.bcbs.com
Blue Cross Canada www.bluecross.ca
GeoBlue www.geo-blue.com
www.treatmentabroad.com A medical tourism site that compares costs of certain treatments between countries.
New Zealand's Accident Compensation Corporation www.acc.co.nz

REQUIRED READING
Health Canada www.healthycanadians.gc.ca
Hong Kong www.expatmedicare.com/healthcare-hk
Italy www.internationalliving.com/countries/italy/health-care-in-italy/
New Zealand www.enz.org/healthcare-migrants-newzealand.html
Sweden www.sweden.se/society/health-care-in-sweden/

CHAPTER 7

RELOCATION 101 | LANGUAGE

"The idea that children are inherently better learners than adults is proving to be a myth. New research cannot find a direct link between age and the ability to learn. The key to learning as quickly as a child, may be to simply take on certain childlike attitudes: lack of self-consciousness, a desire to play in the language and willingness to make mistakes."
John-Erick Jordan via Babbel.com

SHOULD YOU LEARN the native language of the country you are relocating to? Well, *yes* is the culturally correct answer. While doing so is obviously necessary for full integration, to what degree you will learn the language is an entirely different matter largely depending on how you go about your daily business.

I recall being totally floored by a few young American financiers in Paris years ago. I was visiting my friend Julie, who had decided to do a few post-university years in the city, and these guys, her friends, had not learned a stitch of French. Nothing. At two years in!

I remember thinking, *how lazy!* Right or wrong, I dare say that, while living in central Europe, I came to understand their mentality. Because Prague is quite cosmopolitan, with its bustling tourism industry and large community of expats working in the city, I figured I got lucky not having to learn another language. I did not need Czech for my business so I chose not to take lessons and got by on the basics (*hello, please, thank you, goodbye*). I was already struggling with Italian (my partner's family speaks no English, by the way) after all.

Did I miss an opportunity? Definitely. This was made very clear when we encountered difficulty trying to communicate during road trips outside of the city.

In hindsight, I would have purchased an online language course in Czech as soon as I found out we were moving, and then signed up for a month's worth (at least) of one-on-one lessons upon arrival. If only to make sure my pronunciation of "the basics" was correct.

For the move to Sweden, there was no time to do anything aside from packing, but we were quite excited to find out that the government offers a free Swedish For Immigrants (SFI) program. More on that at www.thenewbieguide.se/.

QUICK TIPS
    A. Know your learning style. Are you a grammar nerd? Do you work best with visual aids, or do you prefer listen-and-repeat exercises - or maybe a combo of both? Consider how to optimize learning before investing in a program.
    B. Use the Duolingo app get started. For business proficiency, hire a personal tutor or find an agency that specializes in cross-cultural communication.
    C. Google the programs available in what is to be your new home base.

D. Check out sites like InterNations.org and see if you can join a group of beginners (or advanced) for casual conversation once you've landed.

E. Dedicate time to your new language and be consistent about it. Download one of the suggested apps so you can engage even while on the go.

STEP X STEP

1. **Your Big Why (and Who)** Having a good reason to learn a language will keep you focused and motivated. For me, I want to learn Italian so I can communicate with Mario's family. Their dialect is Toscano versus Romano or Napoletano so that is something to factor in if you are moving to a country like Italy where, as Mario puts it, "cities that are at least half an hour from each other often have a different way of speaking". If you are learning for business, then that will likely change the pace and areas of core conversation you choose to focus on.

2. **Find A Friend** Whether it's your boyfriend, brother or best friend, having someone to practice with will push you forward. Schedule regular meet-ups, but drill yourself at least 30 minutes every day using an online program like Babbel (very reasonably priced), or purchase and download a course from Pimsleur (more expensive, but it's what the CIA uses so it must work). Just be sure to set mutual goals so you stay on track with your partner. If, like me, you actually live with someone who is fluent in the language of choice, then pick one day a week where you only converse a la mode. Perhaps changing it up with a relevant theme or topic.

3. **Relax...Have Fun With It** Kids don't care if they make mistakes so follow their lead. Go for it, fall down, and get back on the *cavallo*. The more chilled out you are, the more you will learn. No pressure.

4. **Leave Your Comfort Zone** Getting uncomfortable is probably the key to the language-learning castle. Ordering in restaurants,

and asking general questions while shopping, are important baby steps if you are ever going to be a confident speaker.

5. **Watch & Listen** Closely watching the body language while listening to people speak fluently in the language you are trying to learn is imperative. Like an actor, you can try imitating them. I love listening to Mario talk to his parents every week via Skype, and Italian movies are also an entertaining option. I know a few people who learned new languages quickly through watching films, TV shows and news programs. If you have kids (or not), why not pick up a few Disney DVDs in the language you are trying to learn?

In the end, not only will the locals respect your efforts, but learning their language will give you important cultural insights on the way people communicate.

RESOURCES

Babbel.com Drills for beginners and advanced learners. Great blog too! **Duolingo.com** This slick app is all about motivation and goal-setting. To that end, you can invite Facebook friends into the mix and learn together. Start with the basics or take a placement test if you are further along. Personally love the daily emails sent to remind me to practice. **Foreign Services Institute** Not as flashy as the above two, but the site is updated regularly. Provides loads of free taped courses that can be used to supplement your learning. **Pimsleur Language Technique** Structured to teach every language under the sun. Quickly. **IOR** www.iorworld.com offers language and cultural training. **Government Web Sites** Search for the language institutions that are government funded.

REQUIRED READING

- www.babbel.com/en/magazine/learn-language-like-a-child

APPS

Babbel Download on the Apple Store or get it on Google Play
Duolingo Available for iOS, Android & Windows

CHAPTER 8

RELOCATION 101 | HOME HUNTING

A SUCCESSFUL HOUSING search depends on a lot of variables, and those variables don't remain constant from country to country. In Prague, we had to go through an agent and pay a full month's rent in commission... for doing pretty much nothing. The whole jam was a surprise to me, but not Mario. Having lived in Florence and Rome, and also having rented in Brussels and Amsterdam, he assured me this was normal practice.

In Sweden, there is really only one web site (Blocket.se) where lodgings are listed and it is common for rentees to post personal ads detailing what they are looking for in a home. It is competitive. Renters want to see that work contract and a social ID number.

If you are lucky, and have an employer assisting in these matters, then all you need to do is make sure the relo department knows the type/ size of accommodation you need. Doesn't hurt to do a little research and request specific neighbourhoods. If they are not involving you in the process, get involved. Ask for updates and links to the properties under consideration and make it clear that you would like to have final sign off. This way you know exactly what you will be walking into.

Even better, if it's within your budget, fly out and have yourself a little orientation trip. We had time to do this for the move to Prague, and it was worth seeing how the city is laid out (Prague 1, 2, 3 etc.) and getting a sense of what the different districts offer. However, trust, this was not done at anything resembling a relaxed pace. We were on a mission; we were in and we were out, and within a week we had signed the lease on a furnished flat in Praha 3. Lucky? Very. The point here is *be prepared to hustle and make decisions quickly.*

We did not have the luxury when moving to Uppsala and, once again, the hustle was on.

Quick story that underscores the "get involved" bit: When we moved to Sweden, the HR department at Mario's company put us in a temporary apartment, which was fine. A bit small, but modern and the location was good. However, the place was on the market and actually sold a few days after our arrival. Not to us. Suffice to say, the apartment we thought we would have for two or three months was not to be... And we were left to scramble to organize new accommodations on our own. The lesson here is that we should have known a start-up company would not be so skilled in handling our relocation. Balls will be dropped so, again, be aware.

STEP X STEP
1. Understand the renting or purchasing protocol, and the level of difficulty that the average expat might have wherever you are going. *What will be required to set yourselves up? What do landlords expect?* Looking into the rules and regulations will often dictate the amount of time one requires to get the job done, and who

is going to assist in the process. If possible, lean on the HR department of the company that is relocating you (or your partner) for as much information as possible. Otherwise, try to pick local brains in the appropriate Facebook group.

2. Whether or not you are planning a recon trip, start doing some research in order to get your (virtual) bearings and become familiar with which areas of the city will meet your needs and match your price range.

3. Going to check things out in advance? Skip staying in a hotel. Use Airbnb or Vrbo and see what your top neighbourhoods have to offer. Selecting a rental (or two if you feel like skipping around) is your best bet on feeling something like a local.

4. This may seem obvious, but don't even consider buying property until you are good and settled, and know you are staying for a significant amount of time.

5. In my experience, it makes sense to rent a furnished apartment. We almost rented a completely empty space in Prague and, looking back, I can't imagine doing that place up and leaving just over a year later. Not worth it. Plus, an unfurnished flat can be overwhelming and you risk over-spending to fill it.

6. Even if you detest the fixed décor, you might be surprised at what a few throw rugs, plants, art and accent pillows will do. After a couple of quick trips to IKEA Prague we were done. Remember, things can change so keep it simple wherever possible.

7. Most important: Get it in writing. If your rental contract needs to be translated, do so before signing. Then make sure all the details are in line with local (and legal) regulations.

Other Notes on Home Hunting Abroad

- Rental Agreements. In Europe, usually there is an extra 50–150 euros tacked on apartments that are already furnished. Although we paid less than 50 euro in Prague - likely because the IKEA furniture was circa 2007 collection.

- Agents. While it is common in Europe to have to pay an agent a full month's rent, plus first and last, renters in Hong Kong will often ask for a security deposit equal to two, or even three, month's rent. Management fees not included. Read up on what to expect where you are going.

- As mentioned, in Sweden things are a bit different. Where I would never consider a personal advertisement to find an apartment, it was recommended we do so. Turns out that, due to high demand, a lot of listings do not actually make it online and landlords are the ones scouring the listings. Since they are anxious to find good tenants, one has to turn on the charm to make a personal ad standout. Yes (gasp/eye roll) photos of the happy couple are suggested. Oh, and then there is the small issue that perhaps one will soon have to do it all over again as leases for more than one year are hard to come by.

- If you have a pet, don't mention that on your personal ad, or in your first communications with a prospective landlord. From experience, I recommend waiting until you are in the door before mentioning the furry facts. Once he or she sees you are the perfect tenants, they will (hopefully) be more agreeable to allowing animals.

RESOURCES

Zillow.com US Real Estate and Rentals

AreaVibes.com Scores US cities based on their livability (cost of living, crime rates, education, employment, etc.)

Lovely US only. Includes Craigslist sources and rental applications are taken through the site. App is available for free on iPhone and Android

Tempaper.com Removable wallpaper, anyone? Fantastic idea for those in a Step #6 situation.

RELATED READING

- **Sweden** www.work.sweden.se/plan-your-move/finding-a-home/
- **Hong Kong** www.justlanded.com/english/Hong-Kong/Hong-Kong-Guide/Housing-Rentals/Rental-contracts-in-Hong-Kong
- **Australia** www.austay.com/rent-a-flat-house-in-australia
- **Best Real Estate Apps of 2020** www.thebalance.com/best-real-estate-apps-4163003

CHAPTER 9

RELATIONSHIPS | FAMILY, FRIENDS & SOCIAL MEDIA

FOR THE LOVE of Grandma Gene, do not announce your big move on social media. Do it and people will undoubtedly be offended that you either didn't pick up the phone, or tell them face-to-face over a celebratory glass of wine. Once you've checked all the major players off the list, then update your Facebook status, tweet, Instagram, make an inspiration board on Pinterest... I don't care. Whatever floats your boat. Have fun - you're about to take off on a transformational adventure!

FAMILY & FRIENDS

Aside from your own emotional junk, some in your inner circle might react as though you are abandoning them (because they see your move away as *all about them*). This is a comfort zone issue and you may encounter a vast range of opinions and perhaps some passive-aggressive behavior. If this happens, it is imperative that you do not take on any sort of guilt. Fear of change is what is really at play and the reality is that they just don't understand why anyone would pull up their roots. While I'm not saying that to belittle anyone's perspective, that kind of reaction can be tough on someone's positive conquer-the-world outlook. Only you can decide if other people's attitudes are going to hold you back. I say it's best to put distance between yourself and whatever is blocking your happiness. Doing so may feel a bit selfish at first, but this is the path to personal growth.

Mitigate these situations by standing your ground and getting clear on boundaries, as well as what you will tolerate.

I am a firm believer that there are 'forever friends' and people that are meant to come in and out of our lives. For better or for worse, each and every relationship will teach us a valuable lesson. Be open and willing to learn, let go and move forward. There will be plenty of people who are very willing to support you once you open up to a new world.

That got a little serious, didn't it?

Overall, I do want you to make a plan to keep in touch with your cheerleaders back home. Recommend suspending communication with the unsupportive lot until you are at least six months in as, quite frankly, you don't need any negativity energy while you are getting settled.

If you don't have a Skype account, get one stat. This service saved me a ton of money, and it allowed me to keep up with friends and family. Engage (authentically) on Facebook, and send the occasional (thoughtful) email, and you should feel that those special connections are being maintained. Life is busy, but it is important to make an effort in this area. The odd handwritten letter or birthday card goes a long way. Friends will miss you. No one likes to feel forgotten.

SIGNIFICANT OTHER

If you are in a marriage or partnership, and therefore moving with someone, then it's going to get stressful. There will be arguments.

What to keep or donate? When to close the bank accounts?

Little things can trigger big meltdowns.

It's all totally natural and an unavoidable part of the process. Make time to talk it out. You are in this together so just be grateful for each other. Usually most things make a good story in hindsight, so try to find humour in situations that might otherwise bring you to your knees.

But before seeing the 20/20 of it all, here are some ideas to take the edge off:

- Plan a getaway… This may sound counter-intuitive but going away the weekend before you move is not a bad idea. Removing yourselves from the chaos of packing will free your mind.
- Hire a sitter… Get those kids out of your way. If you can't give them to granny or another family member, then hire a sitter to take them to the movies or a park for the afternoon while you organize and pack. Plus, you and your partner might benefit from some alone time. Y'know what I'm saying?
- Cook… Sometimes it's the simple things like making a meal that can help to ground the body and make us feel at ease. I am not talking about anything elaborate here. Spaghetti with homemade pesto is easy enough and can be really comforting after a long day of running around. Even if I am exhausted, I do this because I also find the activity of cooking to be very relaxing. So when things get extra hectic, I plan ahead and make sure to get in a grocery shop to purchase whatever I need to prep (or for Mario to make) a delicious dinner in the evening.

FINDING YOUR PEOPLE

While speaking at an event in Toronto, I was asked, *what is the biggest lesson you have learned about yourself in transitioning between so many countries?*

And I answered: *that I am evolving.* That it's OK to take a wrong turn on the road. Recover. Learn. Create something new. Align with supportive people. I do find 'my people' a bit easier now. I know the yoga community is the best place for me to start and build out. It was difficult to really settle in Prague because there was a language barrier to connecting with that group. However, in Sweden, because that barrier does not exist, I was able to integrate quickly and feel more confident about creating a home and a community starting with that yoga base.

More Facebook...

I know you probably have the same love/hate relationship with the Face that I do. My whole perspective on the platform changed when I moved abroad. At the same time, I counted on it more to keep updated with my close friends and family, I also became frustrated by whatever algorithms are used to show posts from the same people, and often days old. So I took a break. Not seeing the point of having 800 "friends" anymore, I shut down my profile and opened a fresh one a couple of months later.

A note if you ever do this… Post an update that you are taking a break about a week or two before you actually suspend or close your profile. This avoids any speculation that you've 'un-friended' people.

Where Facebook does excel for expats is through their groups. Joining an already organized group of local nationals can be beneficial. Because the Italians are just so damn social, Mario always joins the 'Italians in [insert city here]' group and, while he admits he has met some real idiots, he has also linked up with world-class artists in his field and made solid friendships. Something to consider for the advice, and as a way to fast track your knowledge on a place. Here's hoping Zuckerberg won't find a way to charge for it.

SKIP TO CHAPTER 17 FOR MORE ON NETWORKING & RESOURCES

APPS
Skype My favourite. Free on Android and iPhone.

WhatsApp Admittedly I have friends that have been trying to get me to use this for years. Only hear good things about this app that lets you SMS with end-to-end encryption for free. In addition, users can create groups and send unlimited images, video and audio messages.

LINE Messaging, voice and videos calls. Free for all of the same devices as WhatsApp, plus your PC or Mac.

CHAPTER 10

RELATIONSHIPS | THE CHAKRA EFFECT

"After moving to Thailand, I realized that living in fear of change was just causing me to be so unhappy and a very unpleasant person to be around. The Thai people really gave me a reality check. Basically, I wanted some of what they were having. And that is a simple, happy, content life. Even those with very little have this disposition. You really feel it as a deep ingrained thread. With regards to yoga, I have found kundalini to be my favourite because my mind wanders too much so I like the deep focus on the chakras. I have noticed a marked improvement with my practice since I started meditating... I think living in Buddhist culture forces you to stop and consider that staring at your belly button for a period of time might be the key to happiness." *Anne-Marie Bodal*

IT'S TIME TO get a little spiritual. Stay with me here because you might just learn a little ancient wisdom that provides some pretty solid strategies for dealing with the stress that invariably arises before, during and after a big move.

No matter how strong you might think you are, your core sense of self is going to be disrupted. The best thing you can do is be your own light. To know that, no matter what, you can come back home to yourself and find peace. I am not talking about walking around as if the world is a blissful wonderland. That's not realistic, nor advisable for anyone wanting to fully participate in life. Let's talk about finding balance, being resilient, and seeing the lesson in every obstacle. These are core qualities for any Big Mover to cultivate.

On average, we humans spend a lot of time feeling overwhelmed by all the things going on outside of ourselves. Every damn day we face an incredible amount of variables that we have no control over and, as one can imagine, going through the motions of relocation can and will compound stress in the body. Such pressure can manifest in ways that range from general unease, to nervous tension, to developing negative habits to cope. And if you already had these issues then they may get worse. We don't want that. We want your move to be a positive and powerful transformation.

STAYING CENTRED THROUGH THE BIG MOVE
Taking care of our mental and physical well-being is the best health insurance.

And for this purpose, I encourage anyone and everyone to try restorative/yin/slow flow (there are several names for it) yoga, and also to find a form of meditation that adds calm and quiet reflection to the day. It's really not complicated, but it is very much an individual journey to discover the inner awareness tools that will not only fit into your life, but the ones that produce the desired outcomes. All the practice asks is that we do the exact opposite of what is driving us crazy, which is to stop running around like mad trying to make sure everything is perfect.

When we sit in stillness, we actively rest the body and mind, blood pressure naturally drops, and we can focus (if only for a minute) on clearing out the junk (fearful, negative thoughts) to make space for positive messages and perhaps even feel grateful for what is actually going our way. It's so important to have a feel-good revelation once in a while, right? Relocation or not, we can all benefit from building this mental muscle. So get ready to focus on inner peace and feel at home wherever you are!

AWARENESS IS EVERYTHING

So, there I was. Open and willing to make all this change but, having cut the cord to a strong social network in Toronto, I was all of a sudden feeling very lost and alone. I do believe that we develop relationships with the places we live in and me leaving, after almost 20 years, was more like a drama-fueled breakup than conscious uncoupling. Suffice to say, a lot was going on in my head and I desperately needed to find my way to a calm, clear mind. I needed meditation in a big way.

Before moving to Prague, I was fully committed to restorative yoga (which is quite meditative on its own), but I did not have a daily meditation practice.

Side note: I had started to delve into the chakras during my yoga teacher training, and was fully fascinated by the clues this system provided on deep-seated emotional issues. However, it wasn't until I realized how much the big move had shifted my sense of self – physically, emotionally, and environmentally - that I began benefitting from sitting in focused silence.

As luck would have it, I found out about an online series, produced by Oprah and Deepak Chopra, called *Finding Your Flow*. This ran for 21 days through April 2014 and completely flipped the switch. By fixing attention on the seven chakras, I was able to bring some clarity to my dark clouds of indecision and insecurity. The whole jam had such a profound effect on me that I was teaching chakra restorative yoga workshops by March of 2015. But let's back up a bit.

THE SHORT STORY ON THE CHAKRAS

In India, *chakra* means *wheel,* and refers to a spinning vortex of bioenergetic activity. Just like the Chinese use meridians to create a body map, there are seven chakras running up the spine. Each chakra reflects a basic right (to feel, to act, to love, etc.) and each is associated with particular functions of the nervous system, as well as with specific life issues and the way we deal. As spinning wheels of spiritual energy, chakras often become blocked by tension and low self-esteem. When external situations and internal habits throw a chakra off balance, we start to show either deficient or excessive characteristics. For example, there is a sense of being physically and emotionally closed down in the area of a deficient chakra. Excess usually equals overcompensation or addiction.

For those more inclined to side with western science, know that adaptation in the face of stressful situations is called 'allostasis' or 'maintaining stability through change'.

You may have heard of the "allostatic load". If not, to simplify, this is the general wear and tear on the body. When we humans are exposed to repeated stressors, this load increases and the main hormonal mediators of the stress response, cortisol and epinephrine (adrenaline), basically get burnt out. This can lead to adrenal fatigue, which I've suffered from. Not fun and it was a long road back to homeostasis and feeling balanced in mind and body.

Either way you look at it, moving to a brand new place can bring on a sh*t tonne of stress. For the purposes of this guide, we are going to concentrate on the FIRST, SECOND and THIRD CHAKRAS because these relate to grounding and stability in our physical world. Note that the heart is at the centre of the chakra system, and the three chakras above connect us to the spiritual world.

All seven chakras are covered on the cheat sheet in the WORKBOOK available at www.howtomakebigmoves.com.

You can talk to your ND or GP about allostatic load, but I do believe that a basic awareness of the chakras, when combined with yoga and meditation, can greatly help to reduce stress. There's no question these modalities helped me.

GETTING BACK TO CENTRE
Here are the main points on each of those three lower chakras as they relate to pulling up roots for a big move, and the deficient/excessive characteristics that may be triggered. These notes are not meant for any kind of diagnosis, but merely to provide awareness around the issues that may cause you to feel crappy (ie. unbalanced).

The following is common knowledge about the chakra system. How the chakras relate to relocation is my own interpretation.

1ST CHAKRA | *AT HOME IN THE BODY*
Name... Muladhara (Root)
Basic Right... To Be / I Am
Represents... Foundation
Location... Base of Spine (first three vertebrae)/Pelvic Floor
Demon... Fear

Core Issues Connected to Relocation... Money (moving expenses), Family (leaving them behind), Safety (unknown city or country) & Boundaries (maintaining comfortable and appropriate space)

Deficient vs. Excessive... All the things that are part of relocation - travel, being organized – can trigger the anxiety and fear that are related to first chakra deficiency. Restlessness and poor focus may be among the smoke signals. Signs of excessiveness in the first chakra include fear of change; hoarding of possessions or money; attempting to ground the self by gaining a lot of excess weight.

Energy Balanced Around... Paying attention to our survival needs; establishing a healthy sense of security; activities (exercise, yoga, massage) that encourage physical and emotional grounding. Letting go of fear.

Colour / Supportive Foods... Red / Apples, Berries, Radishes

Element / Supportive Foods... Earth / Garlic, Potatoes, Turnips

Moving Mantras... I am safe and secure and the earth supports me. I release my fears through my breath.

2ND CHAKRA | GO WITH THE FLOW

Name... Svadhisthana (Sweetness)

Basic Right... To Feel

Represents... Movement and Connection

Location... Lower Abdomen (below navel)

Demon... Guilt

Core Issues Connected to Relocation... Movement (to a new place), Emotions (go with the flow), Intimacy (connection to others) & Desire (to create)

Deficient vs. Excessive... Symptoms of a second chakra deficiency include resistance to change, fear of pleasure and poor social skills. Sexual problems and discomfort in the lower back, hips, and reproductive organs can also signify that this chakra needs some attention. If any of this rings true, ask yourself: *What can I let go of to live more in the flow and accept my life as it is?*

Excess in this energy centre manifests as strong emotions (mood swing, anyone?), oversensitivity and emotional dependency.

Energy Balanced Around... Graceful movement; ability to change; experiencing physical and emotional pleasure. Letting go of guilt.

Colour / Supportive Foods... Orange / Carrots, Sweet Potatoes, Oranges

Element / Supportive Foods... Water / Coconut or Lemon Water

Moving Mantras... I move through my day with ease and grace. I let go of guilt with every breath.

3ᴿᴰ CHAKRA | *POWER BALANCE*

Name... Manipura (Lustrous Gem)

Basic Right... To Do

Represents... Inner Power & Transformation

Location... Around Navel (up to breastbone)

Demon... Shame

Core Issues Connected to Relocation... Energy (moving forward with enthusiasm), Self-Esteem (confidence) & Proactivity (resolving problems)

Deficient vs. Excessive... As an odd-numbered chakra, this energy centre is aligned with the "masculine" effort of asserting our rights (to have, to ask, to speak, and to know). These chakras tend to move energy through our systems, pushing it out into the world and creating warmth and heat. The even-numbered, "feminine" chakras cool things down, attracting energy inward. So it's no surprise that, in our crazy modern world, masculine and feminine principles are out of balance. The masculine energy of action and expression often overrules the feminine energy of wisdom and acceptance, causing more stress in our lives. The challenge is to use personal power in a balanced manner.

Low energy, low self-esteem, being passive, or playing the victim, can all be indications of a deficient third chakra.

Perfectionism, anger, hatred, and too much emphasis on power, status, and recognition reveal an excessive third chakra.

Energy Balanced Around... Self-esteem and the power of transformation. A healthy third chakra supports our "get-up-and-go" attitude so that we can take risks, assert our will, and assume responsibility for our life.

Colour / Supportive Foods... Yellow / Pineapple, Squash, Bananas

Element / Supportive Foods... Fire / Ginger, Turmeric, Cinnamon

Moving Mantras... I radiate powerful peaceful energy. Shame is not my game.

One can start to see how a big move can throw a person's GROUND, FLOW and POWER out of alignment. When any type of chakra imbalance occurs, the mission is to return to basic body awareness in order to heal and eventually ground our whole selves in the (new) earth. The goal is to feel at ease, confident and peaceful.

Sounds good right? So now you are wondering, *how in holy heck do I get there?*

Read on!

1.A. First Chakra Yoga – Through poses that stretch the back of the body – the legs especially – we benefit from receiving calmness, patience, and a willingness to slow down and stay in one place. Spending time in easy poses like MOUNTAIN (Tadasana) and CORPSE (Savasana) help ground your body. Five minutes is all it takes!

1.B. First Chakra Meditation – It's really not so difficult to meditate. Find five minutes to get yourself in a comfy, seated position close your eyes and repeat (either out loud or mentally) *LUM*. This Sanskrit mantra is directly related to balancing your first chakra. You may also want to use the affirmation suggested above. Imagine a warm red light radiating from the base of your spine while in the pose.

73

2.A. Second Chakra Yoga – Any forward bending pose, with the legs in gentle hip- and groin-opening positions, supports freedom of movement in the pelvis. I'm a fan of PIGEON pose and always get my workshop students in this one to encourage adaptability and receptivity. A simple standing forward fold works too!

2.B. Second Chakra Meditation – While in one of the above poses, or in an easy seated position, repeat the mantra VUM out loud to feel the vibration it creates in the body. Envision a comforting orange glow spreading across your pelvic area.

3.A. Third Chakra Yoga - When you feel disempowered or in need of re-energizing, third chakra poses restore vitality so that you can move from the strength of your core. Practice Surya Namaskar (aka SUN SALUTATION) in the morning. A more passive pose is SUPINE SPINAL TWIST (using blanket between legs and arms out in T or cactus). Restorative, passive backbends that cool off the belly's fire act as calming agents for third chakra excess.

3.B. Third Chakra Meditation – Chant the Sanskrit mantra *RUM* to bring balance to this energy centre. Again, the balancing affirmation can also be repeated while in the pose. Visualize a brilliant yellow light radiating from your navel.

Now, in doing all of this, you may not experience benefits immediately, but I can tell you that with repeated (daily is ideal) effort the effects will start to show in various, at times unexpected, ways. Mental blocks will release their grip and you should feel life flowing in a positive direction.

FOODS THAT HELP GROUND, CALM AND HEAL

With the "supportive foods" listed above, I started hinting that fresh food plays a role and Ayurveda goes hand-in-hand with all this chakra balancing business. Learning about this system of medicine was an eye-opening component of my yoga teacher training. There are many principles and practices in Ayurveda, but I essentially want to highlight that there are foods that balance and foods that aggravate; heating the body up, or cooling it down depending on the season. You know when you eat something that doesn't give you good clean energy; you feel sluggish and uncomfortable. Foods that have this effect are fundamentally incompatible with good health and you might want to pay special attention around a big move. Without going into too much detail here, I will suggest a couple of things:

Find out what unique body/mind constitution (called "dosha" for short) you are by taking a quick quiz at www.theayurvedaexperience. com/dosha-quiz/.

- Pick up *Ayurveda: The Science of Self-Healing*. This is a handy guide that not only provides important insight into your specific dosha, but will also inform you on the foods that either help or hinder your overall balance. NOTE: I am absolutely not suggesting any sort of restricted diet. This is easy information to digest and use to develop general knowledge. Put it all in your back pocket!
- Cook. There's something about chopping and letting a sauce simmer. Try an easy peasy tuna pasta or a saffron and mushroom risotto. Both recipes that require very few ingredients by the way.

CREATE AN EASY MORNING ROUTINE

Whether you are a "morning person" or not, the beginning of the day is sacred time. Start things off on the right foot by drinking a glass of warm lemon water and taking 10 minutes to stretch before you shower. These simple steps will help clear your mind and reset your body.

CHARLENE'S MOVE | *A chakra-related reflection on relocation*
At the beginning of my moving process, it was just about geography. It was all happening on the physical level - requiring the movement and organization of stuff both big (visas to ID cards to bank accounts) and small (closets to cutlery). However, by the end - once I had settled in, with my postcode officially changed, and a new local coffee shop found - I realized I had changed my external environment, but my internal landscape remained the same. For better or worse.

The good part was that no matter where I was, I could always align and ground myself through yoga, or a meditative session of simply sitting and being still. Connecting to the earth in these ways signaled to my body and mind that I had arrived. It wasn't easy by any stretch. I think Eckhart Tolle said it best in his book *A New Earth*: "They haven't really gone anywhere. Only their body is traveling, while they remain where they have always been: in their head."

What was my biggest lesson learned? Don't expect that relocation will be a silver bullet solution to re-inventing yourself, changing up your life, and letting go of baggage. Spending time doing the work of rewiring old thought patterns will serve you better than changing your address.

And if you do go, ease into your new routine and try out different ways of finding calm in chaos. It could be a walking meditation, or sitting quietly with a coffee and your headphones. It doesn't matter what it is; only how it makes you feel. Return to this space when the churn of life threatens to overwhelm.
Ling (Charlene) Lo

RESOURCES

- **Meditation** Recommend downloading the 21-Day *Finding Your Flow* series (www.chopracentermeditation.com/store). There are others as well, but I found this one to be particularly useful as it deals directly with the seven chakras.
- **Happify.com** Information and activity tracks that aim to improve mental flow and help you gracefully deal with everyday challenges.
- **www.oneOeight.tv** With a focus on inner healing, this platform offers loads of videos covering everything from yoga classes with renowned teachers, to healthy food prep, to grief counseling and advice from body image experts. It is a subscription-based resource, but you can sign up for a free 10-day trial period.
- **Ayurvedic Dinner Ideas** www.chopra.com/ccl/the-vedic-chef-3-gourmet-vegan-ayurvedic-dinner-dishes
- **Chakra Restorative Workshops** I teach these so feel free to contact me for more details.

REQUIRED READING

- *Ayurveda: The Science of Self-Healing: A Practical Guide* by Vasant Lad
- *May Cause Miracles* by Gabrielle Bernstein
- *Eastern Body, Western Mind* by Anodea Judith. This is a comprehensive reference book for the person that wants to go deep on the seven chakras.
- Eating for Your Doshas www.goop.com/ayurveda-how-to-eat-for-your-dosha

APPS

- **Buddhify** Incorporate short meditations into your day. Available on iTunes and Google Play.
- **Stop, Breathe and Think** Customizes meditations to your daily emotions. Available for iPhone and Android and also at www.stopbreathethink.com.

- **Relax Melodies** Waves, birds or rain… or all three together. I use this app while traveling to drown out chaotic city sounds and put my mind at ease. Available for iPhone and Google Play.

CHAPTER 11

MAKING THE BIG MOVE |
SELLING YOUR STUFF

SO YOU'RE READY! This chapter is designed specifically to sell stuff and there is a dedicated checklist in my WORKBOOK, which you can download from www.howtomakebigmoves.com and print. The checklist will help you keep track of everything you decide to sell, donate or give to family and friends.

First off, give yourself enough time. Before leaving Toronto, I started sorting stuff and getting my sales channels organized about six weeks before I had to be out of the house we were living in. While I did not have a car or a home to sell, there was still a lot of furniture, kitchenware and décor items, as well as clothing and accessories to unload.

We did not have nearly as much stuff in Prague, so we began preparing about three weeks before moving and made a Facebook event out of it.

We also made sure the prospective new apartment tenants knew what was for sale as well.

Here is a basic timeline to swiftly and efficiently find new homes for your stuff…

4-6 WEEKS BEFORE THE BIG MOVE

- Set up boxes for sorting out what you are hoping to sell vs. what will be given away.
- If taking large pieces of furniture with you, take or have someone else take measurements of doors in your new home to ensure furniture will fit through. If not, find a friend to store it for you or put it on the 'sell' list.
- Take good photos and prepare full descriptions. I neatly staged and shot items as they were in my home (eg. pillows on the bed; full table settings) and used a warm Instagram filter.
- Get your goods on Kijiji, eBay, Craigslist (giving yourself more time if you have larger assets to liquidate). While preparing to leave Toronto, I used my own blog to showcase everything that was going on the block.
- If you don't have a web site, simply create a Facebook event page and invite those you think would be interested in taking things off your hands. I caution against putting this stuff directly on your personal page, as it's not a very targeted approach. You don't want randoms bugging you all day long about whether you think the bathroom vanity will look good in their place.
- Storage. If your relocation is not a permanent one, there may be things you want to hang on to. This is the time to source affordable storage options and/or query friends to see if they are willing to give you some space in their basement.

THE CHECKLIST

- **Making a list of everything you are selling is essential.** Make notes to keep track of who bought what. The last thing you want is to remember you left something in the armoire, but can't recall who hauled it away. Or you know who, but have no way to reach them. Trust me, it gets crazy.

- **Research.** Do a quick check online and see what similar items are selling for.

- **Hire an agency.** If you have big-ticket items like a car, washing machine, or expensive art, then an agent can be a real godsend. They take a commission of course, but if you need to wrap stuff up quickly then look into this option. Not sure? I wasn't either, so I rang up MaxSold.com (available in Canada and USA) and they sent an agent over for a no-charge consultation.

- **Photos.** Take nice photos. I think staging things a bit does help. Take wide and tall shots so people can see how the couch, for example, fits into the room. In my case, I had a charming setup in my coach house so I made sure that came through in the images. Right down to the blender on the counter. This effort paid off.

- **Descriptions.** LxWxH. Make this your mantra and your sanity will be saved, I promise. Measure all items like tables, chairs, beds. Everyone will ask so just put it right in the description online...and write it down on your reference list too so you have the info handy. If you just bought something then say it is brand new. In my case, it was a stainless steel-topped table from West Elm. Whenever someone tried to haggle on the price, I made it clear that "new, no damage" had been stated. That said, be honest about the condition of things.

- **Prices.** Decide the absolute lowest you are willing to go on each item, and then pad all prices with a little room for negotiation. Put yourself in a potential buyer's shoes and be sure it is enough so that the buyer feels satisfied with the final cost. This is not about ripping people off. Rather, this is simply the psychology of the situation. People want a deal.

- **Payment.** Cash only kids. Don't take the risk of accepting personal cheques unless you are dealing with friends (you know where they live, after all). If you actually own your own business then I imagine you could accept credit cards, but if you want to play it safe be firm on cash payment. Don't let anything out of sight until you are fully paid.

- **Security.** Let's be real. Total strangers are coming into your home. I always made sure that either my guy or a close friend was with me. At the very least I knew the landlady was home (I was in a coach house, just a few steps from the main residence). In addition, always keep your smartphone in hand.

Crossing these points off will weed out the lookie-lous or MTWs (Massive Time Wasters) as I like to say. In the end, it was one Kijiji contact that cleaned me out of just about everything from forks and artwork to my bed frame and mattress.

If you take the time to position things correctly, with a little luck and good timing, that one person *will* walk in that just loves your style and wants it all.

Download the WORKBOOK at www. howtomakebigmoves.com and get all the CHECKLISTS & CHEAT SHEETS you'll need for your move!

10 DAYS BEFORE THE BIG MOVE

Have a party! You were going to do this anyway, right? Use this final farewell to get rid of the last few things you have to sell (or giveaway).

In Prague, we created a Facebook event page to invite our local friends over, and to showcase what was still for sale. Some were quick to claim items, while others wanted to have a look at the party.

Some vino, pivo (that's Czech for beer), snacks and boom. Not everything went, but we still had time to push remaining items online. I asked one party-goer if she knew of any good local sites, and she directed me to use the Facebook page 'classifieds.cz', as well as the classifieds section on Expats.cz. Total genius. Within 24 hours I'd sold four major items via Facebook. Not much happened via the Expats ad (which I also boosted to "premium" for about $5 USD)... If you are using sites like Craigslist or Kijiji, it may be worth those few extra dollars to promote your ad.

RESOURCES
Craigslist

Kijiji.ca

eBay

Facebook

www.SabrinasCloset.com Moving your designer goods through this site is simple! Sabrina is based in Montreal, but operates worldwide. **www.hongkong.asiaxpat.com** Useful for selling all major items in Hong Kong.

RECYCLE
For more ideas on how to recycle and where to donate your stuff, check out the dedicated checklist in the workbook that you can download at www.howtomakebigmoves.com.

APPS
VSCO, SnapSeed, Photo Collage... Check out this article for the top editing apps for iPhone and Android www.oberlo.ca/blog/best-photo-editing-apps-iphone-android

CHAPTER 12

MAKING THE BIG MOVE | SHIPPING

"After having given 75% of my possessions to Goodwill, I moved in one large suitcase and two carry-on duffle bags." *Rachel B Velebny*

THIS IS A BIG ONE. I don't know how many F-bombs were dropped in this process, but hopefully I can save you some stress.

Let's review the major pain points...

WHO IS GOING TO GET MY STUFF FROM POINT A TO POINT B?
So now you want to find the most reliable mover and there are a few players in the global freight game.

Start with an online search for 'national shipping services' or 'international shipping' and this will pull up the companies that operate in your part of the world.

You will likely be linked to a web site that acts as a portal offering quotes from three or more shippers with one easy click. I clicked. One got in contact immediately, the second was roughly two weeks later, and the third quote never came. No matter because I was so impressed with the speedy replies to my questions by the first representative that we went with them. Alongside stellar customer service, here are **six things** you want to check before making a final decision:

MOVER vs. BROKER Make sure you are dealing with the mover directly and <u>not</u> a broker. Cutting out the middleman will make sure your quotes are accurate and that you are using licensed movers. If using a broker is unavoidable, just check that they are registered and credible.

CERTIFICATION & AFFLIATIONS Further to the credibility thing, a top-notch moving company will have accreditation with organizations like FIDI, FAIM, IAM and/or BAR.

GOOD REVIEWS Take a bit of time to check that the mover is actually meeting the quality standards that are declared on their web site. Search online, or talk to someone who has recently used their services.

CLEAR COMMUNICATION Understanding all the steps of a successful move can be difficult, so go with the mover that patiently answers all of your questions clearly.

COST EFFECTIVE Obviously.

THE CUSTOMS BROKER Totally different from the broker mentioned above. Skip along to the next section if you are not moving internationally. For those that are, this person essentially facilitates communication between government authorities and importers (you).

They will be clearing your goods through customs when they land by preparing the appropriate documents and calculating taxes and duties. Yes, you have to pay them for this service. And, yes, you will be so much better off choosing a shipper that has solid connections with a customs brokerage abroad. I'll get to why in a bit.

AIR VS. GROUND VS. OCEAN FREIGHT?
Ground and ocean shipments (or a combo of the two) are usually the most cost-effective. For Canada to Czech Republic, we went by sea and it took about three weeks. That being said, air is the best option if you are in a time crunch.

You might be surprised to learn that UPS/DHL/Purolator are not in the business of moving large quantities of personal effects. You can certainly look to one of these companies to ship a couple of "priority" items like computers and framed art, or your Arrival Supplies Box (see chapter on Packing), but don't expect them to handle the rest of it. If you need national ground transport, definitely get a quote from FedEx. They do offer ocean freight shipping between the US, Canada and Mexico.

DO I NEED A CONTAINER (FOR OCEAN FREIGHT)?
This depends on how much stuff you have. The shipping company of choice should advise whether booking an entire container would save you some cash.

WILL MY SUPER FRAGILE STUFF MAKE IT?
Personally, I would never put my Mac desktop computer, or any framed art, on a skid that's going in a truck, that's going in a container on a ship, that's then going in another truck. I have always taken the desktop computer to airline check-in, slapped a fragile sticker on it, and paid for special cargo. Pricey? Yes. (Rates vary based on distance — I paid CDN$100 taking it from Canada to the Czech Republic, and then

50 euro from Prague to Sweden). However, definitely worth the peace of mind and, turns out, it was the right thing to do.

Mario thought I was batsh*t for not packing the Mac with the rest of the boxes, as he did with his own monitor and hard drive. His gear arrived in one piece, but the internal structure of the hard drive (that he had painstakingly built, by the way) had been damaged to the tune of 150 euros. And, to twist the knife, our type of insurance did not cover the cost!

HOW MANY BOXES?
If the shipper is providing the boxes (as ours did for us when we were preparing to leave Prague) do yourself the favour and overestimate the number of boxes. At one month before the big move, either have the boxes sent over, or find a supplier and purchase what you need.

SHOULD I PURCHASE INSURANCE?

The previous paragraph may make purchasing insurance seem pointless, but it's all in the fine print my friend. We're talking "Damage" vs. "Full Loss" vs. "All-Risk". We misinterpreted "full loss" to mean "all covered in all situations", which was absolutely wrong. We were only covered if a box of our stuff completely disappeared along the delivery route. If shipping internationally, you need basic insurance at the very least so make sure you get details on the full range of options and purchase accordingly.

HOW DO I FIGURE OUT THE VALUE OF MY SHIPMENT?

Two important steps that will save time and prepare you for when the shipping company of choice asks for the total value of your shipment:

A. While you are packing, make a list of everything that is in each box. Write it on the outside of the box, or use post-it notes which can then be popped on top before you tape it up.

B. Make a Master List with the current value of each item. Actually, don't make it... Simply download the WORKBOOK at HowToMakeBigMoves.com and get all the CHECKLISTS & CHEAT SHEETS you'll need for your move!

WHAT IMPORT FEES SHOULD I EXPECT WHEN MY BOXES ARRIVE?

As mentioned above, this applies to international shipments and a customs broker should calculate all the charges and taxes.

Note: If shipping within the EU, there are no broker fees.

Get clear on what you will be paying on the other side. Moving internationally is expensive so take a deep breath (remember patience?), suck it up, and budget accordingly.

GO TO www.howtomakebigmoves.com and download the Workbook that has essential CHECKLISTS & CHEAT SHEETS that will keep you organized before, during and after the big move!

STEP X STEP

Honestly, this is something we did not give enough time to understanding on the first round (Toronto to Prague) so, lessons learned, when we had the chance for a do-over (Czech Rep to Sweden), this is how it went down:

1. Asked around for recommendations on international shipping companies and Googled customer satisfaction ratings.
2. Selected a shipper that had professional designations and global affiliations so we knew they were not just sending our stuff off into the ether and hoping for the best, which was our previous experience.
3. Shipped when absolutely everything was packed and ready to go. The first time around we sent two separate shipments - one when Mario left in October and another in December when I left Toronto. For so many reasons doing this was a financial and physical drain so it is infinitely better to send a shipment in one load.
4. Had a conversation with the shipping company's contact in order to be clear on their processes and payment policy. When are payments due and what method is preferred? Some (even the global guys) don't accept credit cards at all. Also, currency may be an issue - in Canada, we had to pay US$ in cash or bank draft.

Note: When shipping out of North America and your shipment is worth more than US $2000, a B13 Export Declaration needs to be completed by you. See FedEx.com for more on that document.

STORY FOR YOU...

In Canada, we used a shipping company (that shall remain nameless here) and they provided a service that was relatively pain-free. Until our shipment got to the Czech Republic, that is. Why? Well, we asked about the fees we would be charged in Prague, but they really had no clue about the associated costs, despite saying we were dealing with their "partners". We just figured this was normal and we got nailed.

Let's just say there was a lot of confusion around customs brokers and charges once our stuff arrived. When all was finally paid and done, this "partner" shipping company told Mario, "We tell the Canadians all the time that we charge a lot to deal with customs on small shipments. It takes quite a bit of time and we have to bill for that." Ugh.

Thing to remember: Usually shipping companies, customs brokerages and the like, are located near airports and not easy to get to without a car. That being said, you may be challenged when you are just arriving. And to have it all sent to your door can be tricky because you have to remit payment and sign documents before the packages can be released.

Mario had to find someone to drive him one hour out of Prague, "to the middle of nowhere" (he still can't talk about it without yelling) to sign, pay and pick everything up. Thankfully he makes friends quickly.

Lessons:
#1 Ensure the shipper you use has good intel on what happens on the other side. And then have some reserve funds handy for the unexpected.

#2 Shipments are usually charged by the square metre so it's best to send everything at once. Due to Mario leaving for his new job before all the packing was done (and I could not get my head around having to handle piles of boxes on my own), we had two shipments. In hindsight, this was a dumb move and we wasted quite a bit of money.

#3 If you are moving to a country where English is the second (or third) language, make nice with a bilingual local. The customs agents may not speak English, so a translator will certainly make things easier on everyone.

Q&A WITH MIRKO AT AGS MOVERS

Mirko Marino was our contact for the shipment we sent from the Czech Republic to Sweden.

Q Is there something we could have done to pay less import fees on our shipment from Toronto to Prague?

A *When I send shipments to other continents, I know how much export customs clearance costs, so I bill my customers accordingly. Then it depends on the rules each country applies for export/import.*

Q Could we have used AGS to ship from Toronto to Prague? If so, would that have saved us time and aggravation? Would we have known the total cost upfront?

A *Yes, you could definitely have used AGS to move from Toronto to Prague. If you had contacted me, I could have arranged your door-to-door move from Toronto to Prague. In Canada I would have used a partner to perform the origin services (packing-out, pick-up and freight to Europe) and then AGS Prague would have taken care of your personal items from the port/airport of arrival in Europe to destination. I would have been in charge of the whole door-to-door and would have clearly advised you in advance about the inclusions/exclusions of my quote. Exclusions are generally all the unforeseeable or force majeure events, such as port congestion, customs inspections, bonded warehouse etc. All those events depend on third parties and moving companies cannot influence.*

Q Another example: Shipping from EU to USA or Canada... Do you have partners there that help determine the full costs of moving for your customers?

A *Of course, in the countries where we do not have branches, like the US or Canada, we have partners who give us the costs for import customs clearance and delivery services. It is the duty of every moving company to clearly state what is included or excluded in their quote, so that the customer clearly knows in advance that there might be extra charges in case some unexpected events happen.*

ANNE'S MOVE

In London we used one company repeatedly and exclusively as they were quite responsive and very good on the whole. However, in the last move we had two trucks – one to go into long-term storage, and one to move to France. Thankfully, on the morning of the move, my husband insisted on double-checking the trucks. I was so embarrassed that I hid in the car. However, it was a good thing he did because they had sent the wrong truck to South Hampton for storage, and were just about to the send the storage truck to France! In the end this meant we had to delay our departure by a night. With nowhere to stay. They offered us, after a lot of complaining, 100 pounds towards a hotel. So, even with "good" movers, don't be afraid to double check! ***Anne Samulevicius***

RESOURCES
WorldFreightNetwork.com
SeaRates.com
AGSMovers.com
UniGroupRelocation.com
MoveCorp.com
UnitedVanLines.com
RobinsonsRelo.com

APPS
MoveMatch Request a quote in less than 10 minutes. A powerful app that helps with moving self-storage. Free for Android & iOS.
The following are only for packages that one might send separately from a larger shipment:
Avery Universal Package Tracker Compatible with FedEx, USPS, UPS, DHL and more. Free for iPhone & Android
17Track All-in-one package tracking service. The website and apps are translated into multiple languages. Free on iOS and Android.

CHAPTER 13

MAKING THE BIG MOVE | PETS

MICROCHIPPING (ISO STANDARD 11784), banned breeds (and special rules for hybrid breeds), vaccinations (timed perfectly), entering the country via specific airports (not all ports are pet-friendly)...

Know. Your. Sh*t.

The rules for exporting/importing animals are country-dependent and you want to pay very close attention. This section is focused on airline travel with cats and dogs for non-commercial purposes.

Of course, if you are staying on continent, there is the option of either driving, or taking a train. I do know people who drove across Canada (Vancouver to Toronto relocation) to avoid putting their dogs in airline cargo.

TIGERLILY'S MOVE

While you might think I'm a total crazy pants for putting my cat through a relocation, I'm happy to report that she made it and settled in her new home pretty quickly. Honestly, I would not have brought Tigerlily if she could not be in the airline cabin with me. With three connecting flights, it was already a rough ride from Canada to the Czech Republic. I can't imagine her in cargo, with me not there to calm her down.

True: Airlines are improving their pet cargo services. They have always been pressurized, but not necessarily climate-controlled. Even so, the engine noise is still an issue. It comes down to knowing how your pet will deal and choosing the option he/she/you will be the most comfortable with.

Research and/or have a conversation with the airline(s) before you book.

When preparing to leave for Sweden, I wanted to fly SAS to earn a few Star Alliance points, but discovered that Czech Airlines had a more generous carrier size allowance (every inch counts!) so we booked the flight with them.

If you're dealing with a large animal, and have no choice but to place them in cargo, then select an airline that provides climate control from start to finish. You don't want your pet waiting on a hot or cold tarmac while the rest of the cargo is being loaded or unloaded. Pet-friendly airlines will hold animals back in a heated or air-conditioned room and drive them out once it's their turn for loading. Upon landing, they are the first to be unloaded.

Whether your pet is flying in cargo, or as part of your carry-on baggage, you have to book space for pets in advance. Note that fees vary and that most carriers limit the number of pets, so budget accordingly and don't leave this to the last minute.

In the case the airline has reached its max capacity, or they simply don't accept pets, all is not lost. There are many companies who arrange the shipping of pets and you can search www.IPATA.org – this is the web site for the International Pet and Animal Transportation Association.

LOW WASTE TIP | Don't throw away your old litter box and scratching post. Find a cat orphanage and donate these items along with any unopened food. Perhaps a friend can take that half-full bag of doggie kibble?

STEP X STEP
1. Paperwork
Research your home country's protocol for export, as well as the rules imposed by the government of your destination country.

It all depends on where you're headed, but the basic forms to file and pack as part of your RAD (Readily Available Documents) are as follows:

- **International Health Certificate** – signed by Licensed Vet and Official Vet
- **Inoculation Record** – signed by Licensed Vet
- **Non-Commercial Movement of Animals** (two copies in each language required) – signed by Licensed Vet & endorsed by Official Vet
- **Pet Passport** (travel within EU only/this covers all of the above three) – signed by Licensed Vet
- **Proof of microchip registration** – print online receipt from 24PetWatch.com or another registry
- **Invoices** as back-up proof of payment.

Pettravel.com is the most comprehensive resource I have found that not only reviews regulations for over 240 countries, but also provides all the necessary forms for transport.

DO check your government's web site, as you may be able to download some forms for free. In my case, when preparing to leave Canada, I was emailed all the necessary documents when I contacted the Official Port Veterinarian (whose contact information I obtained from my local licensed vet).

Things do get a little complicated if your port of entry is not the final destination. Because I had to take Tigerlily through Germany before reaching the Czech Republic, the Non-Commercial Movement forms had to be completed in German as well. I also had the forms in Czech and, while I was told that this was probably not so necessary, it only cost me an extra $20. After numerous trips to the vet, and spending hundreds on vaccinations and the microchip, why take chances, right?

Moving Within the EU
While the rest of the world seems to deal in fussy piles of paperwork for all the necessary documents, the EU ingeniously introduced pet passports in 2001. These cute little blue books enable animals to travel freely (following procedures, of course) between member countries, while also avoiding the whole quarantine thing. Pet passports can only be picked up from a licensed veterinarian and Tigerlily got one before leaving Prague for Sweden.

2. Vet Visits
Check in with your local vet at least two months before travel. Be aware of the vaccinations required and the waiting periods around rabies shots/boosters. You will always have to vaccinate before departure, but your waiting period will depend on when the previous vaccine expires. For example: Because Tigerlily's rabies vaccine had just expired when we were preparing to leave Prague for Sweden, we had to wait 21 days between the fresh shot and travel. Had her previous vaccine still been valid, the waiting period would not apply.

Get all other booster vaccines up to date before you leave. You don't want your pet to be at risk for any viruses in the new country. Plus, it may take more time than anticipated to find a new vet once you have moved.

Tigerlily also needed to lose a wee bit of weight in order to comply with the airline allowed 8kg (including the carrier) maximum. We consulted with our Prague vet to do this safely and effectively by departure date.

3. Government Certification

While getting all the vet business done before departing Canada, I had to make sure I booked an appointment with the government-appointed Port Veterinarian to get all the paperwork signed. Following that, my documents were only valid for 10 days from the date of issue by the licensed veterinarian until the date of the checks at the EU travelers' point of entry. With the exception of dogs to Finland, Malta, the Republic of Ireland and the United Kingdom, where the echinococcus [that's *tapeworms* in plain English] treatment will be the time-limiting factor for length of validity for entry into the EU (i.e. treatment must occur between 120 and 24 hours of entry into the EU). For the purpose of further movements within the Union, the certificate is valid for a total of four months from the date of issue or until the date of expiry of the anti-rabies vaccination, whichever date is earlier.

4. Carriers & Crates

As I alluded to above, each airline is different with regard to on-board carrier/cargo crate dimensions and total weight. Then the rules change again depending on the actual aircraft (CR9 vs. Airbus 321 vs. Boeing 777). Before buying a carrier or a crate, note the LxWxH dimensions for the airline(s) you are traveling on. Or, as I did, book the airline based on those dimensions.

For pets that have to go into cargo hold, they must travel in a crate that is IATA-compliant, which allows the animal to stand, lie down and turn around comfortably. Food and water bowls (choose metal over plastic) have to be attached to the front door, and must be refillable without opening the door. These are the basics so check the airline's web site and call if you are not clear on the regulations.

5. Feeding In Transit

You want to keep meals to a minimum to reduce the chance of any accidents – especially if the cat or dog is traveling in the airline cabin with you. The main thing is keeping their blood sugar up. Pack a bag of both wet and dry treats that are easy to give your pet. If you've got a layover, definitely pack wet food so they can get proper nutrition and some water in their system. I suggest searching 'Kitten Lady' on YouTube for her helpful *How To Fly With Your Cat* video, which covers prep for long-haul flights.

6. Pack Food

Especially important if your pet is on a specific diet. Popping a few packages of food in your suitcase will save you the hassle of having to shop around on arrival. Always a good idea as it might be late by the time you reach your final destination.

7. Insta-Litter

Further to the above, when we first arrived in Uppsala, finding litter sand at a corner shop was not such a problem as trying to find a proper box as there were no pet shops near our apartment. Not knowing the city at all, we managed to improvise using a storage box.

I used the 20/20 insight for my Sweden-to-Italy move and packed a large flat container, filled (about 1/3 full) with litter, in my luggage.

NOTE: If you're really organized, and it is possible to ship a care package of food and supplies ahead of arrival, put that on your to-do list.

8. Stress Less

If your pet is the anxious type then you may want to try Feliway's travel spray, or Bach's Pet *Rescue Remedy*. The former mimics a chemical that cats emit through the glands on their faces when they are feeling calm. The latter is a natural product that is perfectly safe and effective for small animals. I tested Bach's out on Tigerlily before travel and it totally chilled her out. If this does not seem kosher to you, then by all means chat with your veterinarian. He or she may recommend Acepromazine, which is kind of like Prozac for pets. The milder Diphenhydramine (aka Benadryl) is an alternative. Prescription required. Your call, but know that many pet relocation experts don't recommend such medications because they can hinder the animal's ability to regulate body temperature – especially important if the dog or cat is traveling in cargo. Most pet deaths during air travel are caused by excessive sedation.

ONE LAST TIP | Be kind. Speak to your animal in a soothing voice. Once, after a flight from Frankfurt to Prague, I witnessed a dog being picked up from the special cargo desk - clearly distraught and barking like mad. The woman, well, she just yelled at the poor thing. Let me tell you her bad temper did nothing to pacify that dog. Keep calm and carry on people.

ANNE-MARIE'S MOVE
(And why it's important to keep your pet paperwork in order)

From a lady who has moved several times, and really should have known better, this story illustrates that sometimes you just have to learn the hard way.

When I moved from Singapore to Bangkok it involved moving my boyfriend, our stuff, the cat, and myself.

Somewhere along the line during the move prep, it slipped my mind that I needed to keep all the cat vaccination and customs paperwork separate so that his transport between countries would be trouble-free.

Conveniently, I only remembered this particular point three hours after all of our boxes had been packed up. After phoning the movers in a complete state of panic, the best answer I could get was, "It could be in one of the boxes from the kitchen" and, "Madame are you sure you want us to unpack all your kitchen boxes, there are at least ten, this will incur extra charges and you will be delaying your shipment." My stunned silence prompted, "I assume that's a 'no' then?"

Fortunately, I had a couple of weeks of breathing space, so after frantic phone calls to the vet, the pet relocation company, and fits of worry, I managed to pull together some semblance of official looking paperwork to get the cat through customs.

On the day of the move, new paperwork on hand, I arrived at the airport check in counter, cat in carrier, ready to board our flight. One of the ground staff, who I would suggest was at least 100 years old, looked at my paperwork, shook her head, made comments to her colleague under her breath and then proceeded to tell me, "Do you realize you're missing one of your customs forms, so when your cat arrives in Thailand it may be likely he ends up in quarantine for an indefinite period?" And to top it all, "I'm not sure if we can permit him to travel."

To cut a long story short, after more panicked phone calls to the pet relocation agency eventually we were allowed to board the flight. Holding my breath, we arrived at Bangkok airport and literally sailed through immigration with no issues. Thank goodness! However, with just a bit of advanced planning and smart packing, I could have saved myself stress, time, and few grey hairs. *Anne-Marie Bodal*

RESOURCES
IPATA.org
Feliway.com
PetRelocation.com International pet shipping service
PetTravel.com Worldwide resource for travel with pets (including airline pet policies)
24PetWatch.com Pet insurance and microchip registration (USA & Canada)
Europetnet.com Microchip registration; lists member organizations by country
Canadian Food Inspection Agency www.inspection.gc.ca
United States Department of Agriculture www.usda.gov
European Commission www.ec.europa.eu/food/animals/pet-movement/eu-legislation/non-commercial-non-eu_en
U-pet.co Soft-sided carriers made from non-toxic materials, with cute cosmonaut-style windows.
Pettravelstore.com A variety of products, including crates for cats and dogs, plus instructions on how to measure your pet.

REQUIRED READING/WATCHING
- International Air Transport Association (IATA) www.iata.org/whatwedo/cargo/live-animals/pets/PAGES/index/aspx
- Atlas Van Lines www.atlasvanlines.com/moving-tips/how-to-move-guides/moving-pets
- Pet Travel Routine: Flying with a Cat www.youtu.be/NRvc-2P7syQ

APPS
MyPet Reminders Keep track of your pet's personal info, including vaccinations and vet appointments. Free for iPhone & Google Play
Pet First Aid by the Red Cross Advice for everyday emergency situations for cats and dogs. Free for Google Play

CHAPTER 14

MAKING THE BIG MOVE | PACKING/UNPACKING

I THINK I would rather ...well, there are a thousand things I would rather do than pack. I feel your pain. I will start by saying that if you put a lot of effort into selling/donating your stuff, then this stage of the big move will be miles more manageable. Continue to make de-cluttering your M.O. Recycle or giveaway what you don't need. There will be stuff to garbage so just be sure to shred any sensitive documents, like old bank statements for example.

SUPPLIES
Boxes – *either have your shipping company deliver them or make arrangements to get boxes from a local retailer.*
Bins
Newspaper
Bubble wrap
Packing Tape Gun

Large Plastic Bags – *for garbage and to use to line boxes*
Large and small Ziploc bags – *handy for packing everything from toiletries to toys. Ziploc also makes large flexible totes that are great for bedding.*
Camera
Post-It Notes
Tabs *(to label electrical cords)* – *either use the ones that come on packages of bread or colour code with those sticky ones made by Post-it®.*
Marker & Pens

DIVIDE AND CONQUER

When it came to packing, honestly it was far better for me to go it alone. Let's just say I'm way more "on it" than my guy. That's not to say he did not do his part in packing up his own clothing and computer stuff, but bathroom, kitchen, etc... Perfectly fine to leave it to me. It's just about time management, and he was better being directed to sort out the technical stuff (like dealing with returning the WIFI modem) or cleaning (Mario is very good at changing vacuum bags) and taking out the recycling.

My point is, if there are others involved in your move, then assign tasks that make sense for each team member and set clear deadlines.

STEP X STEP (IT'S A BIT LIKE TETRIS)

You are going to take this room-by-room; starting with the items you don't need in the weeks prior to departure. Dedicate a day to each room and plan out, on a calendar, how many days it's going to take you. Keep in mind some rooms may require two or three days to pack up.

Budget your time accordingly.

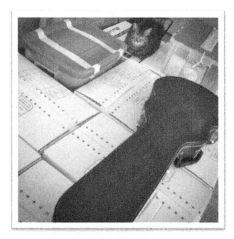

1. Set up your boxes or plastic bins – placing them all on the ground floor if you're working with an upstairs and a basement. Better to bring the books to the box than the other way around. Think ahead. Save your back.
2. Designate boxes for donations.
3. Give each box a number and clearly write it on all sides for easy reference. Trust me this will avoid frustration later on!
4. Line each box or bin with a large plastic bag – garbage or drycleaner – to provide an extra layer of protection.
5. Stick post-it notes on the outside of each box and write what is going in as you fill them.

Need some tunes to get you in the packing mood? Listen to the BIG MOVES playlist on <u>Spotify</u>.

6. When you are all packed, use the Post-its to make one Master List. The Master does not have to be super specific; general descriptions will do just fine. We did not do this on our first go-around (Toronto to Prague) and were scrambling to make our Contents List while at the shipping office. Fail.

7. The last step is to then pop the Post-its on top of the stuff in each box before closing and taping them up. While your Master List will make sure you don't bother opening the "winter clothes" box in June, the Post-its will quickly remind you exactly what's inside when you're looking for the desktop organizer in Box #2.

8. For boxes that have fragile contents and/or absolutely need to be shipped "This Way Up", do mark them accordingly with black permanent marker. In the case that those special boxes arrive upside down, take photos before removing the shrink-wrap as you want Exhibit A for the shipping company should there be any damages. This is what insurance is for, after all.

9. Data backup. Very important to backup your important files. I am a fan of USB keys and external hard drives, but if you prefer using the cloud go for it. A virtual pack-up of your files is not to be skipped so make this a part of your to-do list. I have had situations where my MacBook Air went through some rough travel (read: press trip to Honduras and then a writers' workshop in Guatemala) and she crashed and burned less than a month later. I had grossly underestimated the durability of this Apple product and lost a bunch of really important documents. I mean, have you ever looked under the hood of an Air? Literally taped together. It's shocking and not surprising the laptop did not survive. This is a random story, but my point is that travel is hard on everyone and everything so take the time to secure what is important to you.

10. Arrival Supplies Box. Think: pots and pans, pet supplies, favourite foods, toiletries... Anything that you'll need right away and that will help free your mind. If it's possible for someone to receive this small box of goods so it will be waiting for you, then pack and ship ahead via FedEx, DHL or the like.

UNPACKING

Just as overwhelming as packing, no question. Here are a few tips to help:

- Designate one room for all the boxes. Then, using your Master List, go room by room starting with the most important stuff. Kitchen, bathroom, bedroom, office, etc... Place the box(es) in the associated room and unpack.
- Fragile first. Unpack the boxes with the most fragile contents as soon as you receive the shipment. A sad story for you:

We assumed Mario's PC components – basically a box encasing a super computer that he and a friend had painstakingly assembled together – had arrived in one piece. However, when we finally had a chance to unpack it, almost a month later, it was a shambolic mess. Because of the lag time it was pretty much impossible to get any sort of compensation through our shipping company. Burn.

- Take your time. If you have moved in the summer and you would rather be outside, then push the general unpacking to a rainy day. Or winter. Whichever comes first.
- Of course, nothing speeds up this part of the puzzle like an impending visit from a friend or relative. At least I find this to be an incredible motivator. Case in point: When we moved into our apartment in Uppsala, we were thrilled to have a spare room to store all of the boxes we could not be bothered to unpack right away (it was high summer, after all). It was out of sight, out of mind until my younger brother, eager to meet a Scandinavian princess, announced he would be visiting us in November. At that point we had about two months, and this gave us just the right amount of time to unpack, clean and furnish the spare room without too much pressure.

LOW WASTE TIP | Hang on to good reusable packaging. I especially like IKEA's thick plastic bags and cardboard packaging. Roll up the plastic and gently breakdown the boxes. Keep only what you have enough storage space for.

A few words of sage advice from my friend Anne, who relocated from London to Corsica with her husband and young children.

"Do one thing at a time, not more. If that thing is having fun for an hour on a Sunday afternoon, just do that. If it's organizing the medical file for your family, don't start opening drawers and wondering if you should pack all the paperclips you've inexplicably been hoarding for the last five years. I know, I know, we are all supposed to be multi-tasking geniuses, and you feel like you have NO time, not even the time to read this. But the truth is that multi-tasking is a myth. Your brain can only do one thing at a time. Even if it's what you do at work, or how you survive an evening with kids and laundry and the stuff of life, and it's the only way you have time to fit everything into your average day. Right now you are moving. If you do each thing consciously and calmly you'll be a lot more likely to remember having done it, and how you did it. I promise, being able to clearly remember sending in the tax form, or that you packed the Christmas decorations with the tennis rackets, will save you a lot of turmoil on the other end. Plus, your kids and partner, and pets and friends, will all fare better if they've had the pleasure of your constant attention. Even if the increments are shorter in the upheaval of moving. So be a champion uni-tasker, and take it one thing at a time."

Anne Samulevicius

CHAPTER 15

MAKING THE BIG MOVE | TECH SUPPORT & SECURITY

WE'VE COME A long way from the days of snail mail post and relying on our compass-reading skills to deliver us to the right destination. It's incredible what we can do from our desktops these days. And with everything quickly going mobile, it's easier than ever to be a citizen of the world.

Here are a few technical tips to help you go global:
1. Highly recommend downloading *Google Chrome with Translate* and setting your computer up to use this internet browser as it is best equipped to translate web pages.
2. When it comes to translating life on the go, Google has your back again with their handy translator app. I also used it to take photos and decipher our Swedish mail and newspaper headlines as it's always good to have a sense of what the local issues are.

These apps are helpful when grocery shopping, understanding parking signs, as well as instructions on the washing machine.

TRANSLATION TIP | When you need to translate an entire web site, go to translate.google.com and paste the URL into the left window and, if not auto-detected, click the corresponding language above. The link will automatically pop up in the right window; click on the language you need to read the site in. Et voila!

APPS

There are all sorts of apps for all sorts of smartphones. Test a few out to see which one works best for your purposes. There are amazing apps out there that are specific to your new country or city.

Take Taxi – Hong Kong Taxi Translator (iOS and Android), for example, is one of those indispensable genius apps that acts as a powerful tool to find and translate addresses into Chinese characters and phonetic Cantonese.

Yelp Tens of millions of business reviews worldwide. Free for iPhone and Android

Google Maps Navigation will never be the same. Get comprehensive maps for 220 countries and territories. Free for iOS and Android

Google Translate Type to translate 103 languages, or take a photo and translate text in 90 languages. Free for iOS and Android

TECHNOLOGY & PERSONAL SECURITY

When it comes to personal security, I wrote an article about fraud and identity theft for ~~The~~ Huffington Post and, while researching, I was shocked at the global state of affairs. How do cyber crooks get past the sophisticated firewalls that are supposed to protect us?

From old-school thievery to what's known as "visual hacking", it seems everyone is at risk.

We have all heard about the major data hacks at Sony and the U.S. government, but I wanted to scale it down to what I can do to protect my personal information.

Here's what I have for you after doing the deep dive:

#1 When checking personal information such as bank account or email whilst abroad, always ensure the data connection is encrypted with a password on a secure device. So, while you are enjoying your lazy mornings in charming European cafes, avoid checking your credit balance or making any transfers via public WIFI. Know that credit cards offer more protection from fraud.

Before we had our home internet set up in Sweden, and when I needed to access online banking, I simply set up data on my smartphone and securely networked to the web that way. Same for PayPal and Skype when I was calling banks or airlines, and where I knew I would be giving my credit card details. In the case you are forced to use an unsecure connection, change any online passwords as soon as you get to a secure one.

#2 Further to the above, never select to "save your password" when you are logging in online. If someone gets a hold of your computer, it's over. Destroy old SIM cards, or keep ones you plan to use again in a secure spot.

#3 Google before you go and take extra precautions in cities and countries that have rampant organized fraud. One example is the state of Florida, which frequently ranks first in identity theft cases and makes a significant contribution to the hundreds of thousands of fraudulent tax returns filed every year that cost the US Government billions.

#4 Cities such as Barcelona, Buenos Aires, Hanoi and Prague consistently make Top 10 lists as places to beware of pickpockets. (Did I mention my phone was stolen at a restaurant in Prague?)

In places like these, you would do best carrying cash and cards around in a money belt around your waist, versus a wallet that is loose in your bag. Yes, yes, money belts are a little tourist-geeky, but safety is never a fashion crime.

DATA SECURITY

Don't go crazy thinking you have to change your passwords every month. Consider regularly changing passwords for communication-type sites that don't have two-factor authentication. Think: email, instant messaging or conferencing services. These are more likely to be hacked and the sneaks might be listening for months before you find out.

Some services, including Gmail, Facebook, and Dropbox, show your active sessions. As a general security precaution, you can check those to make sure no one else is logging into your accounts.

TIP | When it comes to shopping abroad, PayPal has linked up with Borderlinx to make it easier to shop from abroad without hidden costs, even from webstores that don't normally deliver to your country. Borderlinx takes care of everything; from the customs process to the delivery of your purchases. Free US and UK delivery addresses are available at the moment.

CHAPTER 16

MAKING THE BIG MOVE | THE
FINAL COUNTDOWN

AT TWO WEEKS OUT, you want to make sure you are doing as much as possible during the day so you can free yourself up to spend evenings with friends and family before you go. Squeeze a massage in there with your favourite therapist, or a session with that other kind of therapist (possibly more necessary).

You need lots of energy so be sure to eat regular healthy meals throughout the day... and don't forget lunches and dinners at your most beloved spots. Schedule it all out baby!

14 Days Make a Master List of all the things that need to be wrapped up. The tasks do not need to be in any exact order. This list is for reference when you sit down to make each 'to-do tomorrow' list in the evening. Doing this every night before you go to bed will help you feel in control and, hopefully, sleep better.

12 Days Go through your stash of medicine and see what has expired. Pack what you want to take with you, then go to your local pharmacy to dispose of those expired medicines and prescriptions, as well as hardware like inhalers.

10 Days Have a few friends over to help say goodbye to the place. This is a good opportunity to sell and/or give them any items that you no longer want.

9 Days Review the contents of your fridge and make a plan to use up the food.

8 Days Don't forget your meditation practice! Stay in the flow. At this point you should be wrapping up any work, as everything will be on hold from your final four days until you settle in your new home. If it's important that you stay active on social media, this is a good time to prepare and schedule posts.

7 Days Plan to get away for the weekend. At the least go for a scenic drive or hike. Whatever gets you and your partner/kids out of the mess of packing for a bit.

6 Days Resist the urge to clean. There is no point until you're done packing and all the boxes are out the door. I mean, do the basics in the bathroom and wash your dishes, of course. People will drop by unexpectedly so contain your hurricane.

5 Days Remain positive. You can do this. Assess your appointments for the coming days and be realistic as to whether you can keep them. In my experience, don't plan to do anything unrelated to your move the day before you take off. Unexpected things ALWAYS pop up that may keep you housebound. Confirm, change, or cancel as needed.

4 Days Final drop at Goodwill or other charity of choice. Canned goods can go to your local food bank. Pick up moving day snacks for everyone, including the pets.

3 Days Write and schedule your 'away' email auto-response to cover those days you will be offline. Update social media accounts.

2 Days This is don't-lose-your-cool time. You might be out dealing with the shipping or storage company, or in doing some of the cleaning.

1 Day Out Close up the boxes and make sure all your important documents are in order. Make sure the suitcases close too – checking that they are not overweight if going by air. Do that final walk through and cleaning.

On Moving Day...
You will become your mother, or father, and perhaps say and do things that are completely out of character. In other words, your biggest bitch will come out over the smallest of problems.

It helps to know your triggers. For me it's cleaning. I can't stand a mess, or anyone thinking I am messy. Example: Our landlady in Prague was particular about the (old, crappy) pots that had been supplied as part of the furnished apartment contract. While going through the checkout process, she did not think we had cleaned them well enough. I scrubbed again. On moving morning, when Mario went to wash those same pots, I lost my mind.

If you find yourself in the same sitch, take 10 deep breaths and carry on. Hopefully whomever you unleashed unholy hellfire on will forgive you.

PREPARATION FOR ARRIVAL

Nothing keeps us organized like a list, but here are a few other things to consider:

Clothing. Are you going from summer to winter or vice versa? Make sure you have easy access to weather-appropriate gear. If you know you need to purchase new boots and such then that's another list.

Power. You need it. Best to purchase adaptors before you leave. Portable battery chargers are a great thing and very handy for long-haul travel. Jackery has both a Giant and a Mini product that go the distance.

Public Holidays. Make note of all the stat holidays in your new country well before you go. Always good to know as you might not want to arrive on one…just saying. This happened to Mario when he relocated from Italy to Holland in the dead of winter. No shops were open. It was a mess.

Hospitals and Medical Care. Find out where the closest hospital is in relation to your new home. In terms of GPs, specialists and dentists, it's worth doing a search so you know where to go. When you are not feeling well, you will be glad to have names and numbers handy for quick reference.

Receipts. Keep all of them and stay on top of amounts owing/owed. If you are with a partner, you may want to divide expenses as one may be putting all the IKEA purchases on her credit card, while he pays the rent.

List the basics for your first shopping trip. You know what you like to eat and drink so write all the things down that will help make a meal in a flash. Cleaning supplies (try to find non-toxic wherever possible) and pet stuff go here too.

TIP| Once you have written out your list, pull up Google Translate and next to each item write the word in the local language. Don't forget the bubbly!

Use the EXPENSE TRACKING FORM & FIRST SHOP CHECKLIST – both in the WORKBOOK available for download at www.howtomakebigmoves.com.

Travel. Do not, I repeat, do not commit to traveling out of your new country for at least two months post-relocation. Aside from the rules (in some countries) around applying for residency, there are other reasons to stay grounded. Just getting settled, for one. You may also have to wait on other documents and deliveries. We left Sweden just a month after arrival in order to attend a wedding in Montreal. Although we were happy to be there for our friends, it took a toll on our energy resources, which had already been maxed out from the move and stress of apartment hunting.

Pets and Vets. Last, but certainly not least, the fur babies will need to see a veterinarian once in a while, so note where the closest one is.

CHAPTER 17

MAKING THE BIG MOVE | NETWORKING
(AKA. GET OFF THE COMPUTER!)

"In changing coasts [NYC to LA], I made the mistake of thinking I'd find a community overnight. I'm personable, right? I'm friendly? It takes time to feel the rhythm of a city, to discover its heartbeat. It takes time to convince new friends you're worth the effort. Don't be so hard on yourself."
Mickey Rapkin

MORE ON FINDING YOUR PEOPLE
This continues the thought from Chapter 9. Whether you join a running club, or sign up for weekly entrepreneurial brainstorms, you need to go where your people are. I know the yoga community is the best place for me to start and build out so that was my first "target market". All I had to do was find a yoga studio that offered the sort of yoga I like to practice and, second, enquire whether I could teach

there. Miraculously, all of this can be done before taking off so apply this to your own situation and set yourself up for success!

I knew I could work as soon as I arrived in Sweden, but even if your work permit is not sorted out, there's no harm in connecting with business owners and start establishing relationships.

Here are more tips to get you in the friend-making flow...

Meetup.com - The world's largest network of local groups. Totally easy for anyone to organize a gathering of like-minds, or join one of the thousands already meeting face-to-face. www.meetup.com

Impact Hub – A well-run entrepreneurial centre that has outposts in several major cities. My experience with them in Prague was very good as the staff really made an effort to help me feel comfortable and they facilitated worthy connections. At present there are over 100 Hubs across five continents and in over 50 countries. www.impacthub.net

InterNations – An international organization that offers professional and social connections via events and workshops. At press time there are 3.8 million members in 420 cities. The membership is tiered, but you can attend events by simply registering and paying a small fee at the door. Highly recommend for connecting with high caliber humans. www.internations.org

Facebook Groups – Search by city, country and/or nationality. Join well before you make your move to cull critical info (always triple checking validity!) and ask questions.

Tours – Go on every city tour that interests you. In a place like Prague there is so much history, art and architecture to take in. Even the beer tours offer interesting insight. This is a great way to meet people too. Albeit they'll likely be tourists, but you can still exercise your conversation-starting muscles.

Language Courses – Worth taking because you are bound to meet others in the same boat.

Teach or Tutor – If you have a talent for music, competency with a particular language, or some other certified skill, then find the best way to share it. It may be possible to volunteer at a local community centre, or perhaps post an ad directed at the expat community (Facebook and other forums) for free group lessons.

Make Sweet Music – By taking guitar lessons, Mario had a nice little micro group going in Toronto.

Work Out – Personally, I think going for a run around your new 'hood is a great way to get oriented. But please, safety first. At least for those initial few excursions, leave the ear buds and whatever you use to listen to music, at home. Especially in cities, traffic rules are so different (and people can be somewhat indifferent to them) and you need to pay full attention. For example, in Prague, car drivers really don't like to slow down at pedestrian crossings. On several occasions I am not sure what would have happened if I'd been in my Jay Z-zone.

TIP | Walking into any situation, you have to think: *I am strong; I am confident; I am a good person and others will see that.* It may not happen immediately, or overnight, or in the first month, but your good energy will resonate and the friend-making will begin!

ASHLEIGH'S MOVE
I moved from Toronto to LA a few years ago with my husband and our three-week old baby. Admittedly it probably wasn't the best time to

be setting up shop in a new city, but I look at the timing as a blessing as well.

Knowing it was essential to my overall happiness, I was determined to build a healthy social life. Despite challenges as a new mother, I took "friend dating" to an entirely new level. I never turned down any opportunity to meet someone - whether it was a coffee via a common friend, a cold call on my behalf, or some sort of social gathering that I received an invite to. That strategy paid off, and after a year in LA, it began to feel like home. I had a solid group of friends, and had navigated my way through the city to a point where I had secured my local haunts. We travel a lot, but now, every time I land back on the LAX tarmac, there is a feeling of comfort.

Overall, I can say the relocation taught me how to build a good community. To have confidence and step out on my own.

It's hard being the new person, but the lesson is simple: the more you put in, the more you get out. *Ashleigh Dempster*

> *Sometimes your only available transportation is a leap of faith.*
> – Margaret Shepherd

CHAPTER 18

FINAL WORDS OF ADVICE

"Bangkok is fascinating. An incredible history, with thousand-year-old architecture, juxtaposed against modern glass skyscrapers barely containing a hot, pumping, forward-moving city. It can be a bit of shock to the system, but I loved it. I think the most noticeable shift for me in comparison to Singapore, and anywhere else to be honest, was living in a Buddhist country. You really do feel this strong thread of goodness and authenticity in the people. And as we all know, in the end, it's the people that make a place." *Anne-Marie Bodal*

Your habits will change. That's the truth. A new environment and culture will ask you to adjust your daily routine. This is a golden opportunity to try new things. Go with the flow and you will find a rhythm that works.

Allow extra time for everything. The reality is that it's going to take more time to find what you need. Navigating a new grocery store can be somewhat maddening. Where are the frozen peas? And why the hell aren't the almonds and pine nuts in the same section? Am I even going to like this unknown brand of fro yo? Give yourself time to process all this new stuff. If you can block the time, so as not to be rushed, the getting-to-know-the-place phase can actually be rather enjoyable.

Don't assume. Do not make the mistake of assuming things will run the same way that they did in whichever country you are coming from. Case in point, in Toronto, when maintenance type things were happening, I was always informed by the management or landlord in advance. With regard to our building in Prague, while notices were posted occasionally, some important things were missed. Like the time they sprayed toxic chemicals on the grass, which could have caused serious harm to our cat if we had, as we were used to doing, let her run around in the garden. There was another morning when workmen were up on the roof, and right outside our bedroom window. Not ideal.
All to say you might want to double check the policy in your new pad and make it clear to the appropriate person that you want to be informed at least 24 hours before things are scheduled to happen.

Recycling and garbage collection. Another area of please-do-not-assume-it's-the-same-deal. I loathe any kind of waste so I was in my happy place in Sweden because they recycle about 90% of household garbage. There are bins for everything, making it super simple for residents. Going steps further, the Swedes actually buy garbage from other countries and turn it into energy. Amazing, right? My main point here is that starting fresh in a new place is a great opportunity to make adjustments and live a life less wasteful.

Use the RECYCLING CHEAT SHEET in the WORKBOOK available at www.howtomakebigmoves.com

Do reach out before you go. About a month before we moved to Sweden, I started casually emailing yoga studios to see if I could set up meetings and/or teach a workshop in the coming months. This is great for establishing a rapport. I had a meeting set in Uppsala pretty much the same day I sent out my query.

Weather. Ladies and gentleman, prepare yourselves. Aside from your routine, the weather will change your skin and hair. Moving from Bermuda's insanely humid summers to Canada's climate was a welcome change. Until the winter brought super dry skin, of course. Things pretty much stayed the same in Prague. However, moving even further north to Sweden, my skin freaked out in the ultra-dry environment. My whole skin and hair care regime had to change to compensate. While I used the same brands, I had to buy heavier creams for face and body, as well as more intense hair conditioners.

My friend Charlene's experience…
"The humidity in Hong Kong was a huge change from the dry climates I was used to in Canada. People forget that this part of China has a tropical climate. It's a big city with smog issues and mountainous topography, which all contribute to relentless humidity in the summer and bone-chilling dampness in the winter. The temperature would be 10 degrees, but it felt much colder. And because there's no inside heating (anywhere!), or proper insulation in the older buildings, this meant that it was colder in my apartment than outside. I slept with a toque on at night! The only good thing was that the humidity did wonders for my too-dry hair in the summer so I mastered the messy "beach" look.

Health. Climate change will affect more than your hair. For example, because of the light to dark ratio drastically changing for us when we moved to Sweden, we had to up our Vitamin D intake. Sun lamps are wise investments in these cases. Down under, my father and brother had to deal with crazy allergies after moving to New Zealand's South Island.

Watch exchange rates. This is critical if you are being paid in your new country's currency, or not. You want to be aware of its valuation at all times. Case in point: Two months after my partner started working in Prague, the Czech koruna lost significant value. He asked for a raise a lot earlier than he would have because of this.

Trips back home. Don't plan too much. Make appointments with the key people and let the rest organically fall into place. I have made the mistake of overbooking myself on a few trips and wind up having to cancel because I am too tired.

Repatriation. Meaning: *The process of returning a person to their place of origin or citizenship.*

Be aware of the people and processes that will help you return easily. If your employer is bringing you back, they should provide the necessary services. In my case, going back to Canada, to a different province (British Columbia) than the one I was living in previously (Ontario), it was still quite easy to reinstate my residency because social insurance numbers (SIN) don't expire. Once we landed, registered for our BC Services cards and got "back in the system", I was able to access healthcare coverage within 90 days. The paperwork was moreso with the Italian consulate in Vancouver as Mario and I had to declare ourselves residents of Canada in order to revoke our Italian residency status. Very important for tax purposes.

If you need to move money around, watch those exchange rates and connect with an accountant and/or the bank you were using before you left.

EASY LISTENING, RECOMMENDED READING & MORE TIPS

Good Life Project's interview with Natalie Sisson - Native New Zealander and champion of the *Freedom Plan*, Natalie Sisson, talks about the realities of location independence and the intricacies of doing business in foreign environments. www.goodlifeproject.com/natalie-sisson/

May Cause Miracles **& Miracle Membership** – Gabrielle Bernstein has many books but *MCM* is my favourite as the profound lessons within have kept me grounded. Her membership portal is brilliant and delivers new content monthly. Gabby's spiritual, yet very practical advice never fails to balance me out when I feel scattered.

Finding Your Flow - This 21-day meditation series produced by Oprah and Deepak Chopra is my saving grace. See Chapter 10 for more if you missed that bit.

Brendon Burchard – This guy is the expert on productivity. His tips and new day planner are extremely helpful and you can find loads of videos at www.brendon.com.

Wall Street Journal Expat – My favourite blog for everything expat is no longer publishing posts, but it's still a great resource. www.blogs.wsj.com/expat

LivingSocial – Discover unique local businesses and niche products through this daily deal site that's live in 27 countries. www.livingsocial.com

LET'S CONNECT

Check out my social media links for more information,

inspiration, supportive suggestions and resources…

Instagram.com/howtomakebigmoves

Linkedin.com/in/saragrahamatfreshpresse

IF YOU ENJOYED THIS GUIDEBOOK, I'D BE VERY GRATEFUL IF YOU COULD PLEASE POST A REVIEW ON THE BOOKSELLER PLATFORM WHERE YOU PURCHASED THE E-BOOK OR PRINT VERSION.

WELL, IT'S BEEN LOVELY HAVING YOU ON BOARD. GOOD LUCK WITH YOUR BIG MOVE!

THANKS TO SOME BIG MOVERS...

This guide would have never happened without the generous support of the following individuals who backed this project via my Kickstarter campaign.

EXECUTIVE PRODUCER
Brian & Carol Graham – New Zealand

PRODUCER
Ted Graham – New Zealand

CO-PRODUCERS
Chuck & Colleen Poulain - Canada
Daniel & Lenka Graham - New Zealand
Julie Kane – Bermuda
Marcus Doyle - Canada
Stephen & Tiffany Graham - Canada

SPECIAL THANKS
Alex Ratteray20!9 - UK
Cathy Poulain – Canada
Hollis Wilder – USA
Jodi Simpson - Canada
Kaaren Whitney-Vernon – Canada
Lindsay Clease – Canada
Lisa LeBlanc - Bermuda
Mario Baldi - Sweden
Stuart Knight - Canada

THANKS

Alejandra De Miguel - Argentina
Amanda Alvaro – Canada
Anne-Marie Bodal - Thailand
Anne Samulevicius - Corsica
Betsy Blankenbaker - USA
Cailey Heap-Estrin - Canada
Caroline Gill – Canada
Danielle Domenichini - Canada
Gil Mangonlat – Canada
Giles Armstrong – UK
Heidi Amos – Bermuda
Karen Cleveland - Canada
Kelsey Malenchak - Canada
Konstantine Malishevski – Canada
Lisa Williams - Canada
Mickey Rapkin - USA
Paul Marchildon – Canada
Paulina Corvalan – New Zealand
Rachel Velebny – Czech Republic
Rachael Barritt - Bermuda
Sarah Kelsey – Canada
Susan Szabo - USA
Thomas Overfield – Sweden

Made in the USA
Monee, IL
05 November 2020